SEED CRACKED OPEN

STORIES OF AN EVERYDAY PILGRIM VOLUME 2

ESTHER HIZSA

Printed and bound by Kindle Direct Publishing in the United States of America

"Seed Cracked Open", "Two Giant Fat People", "With that Moon Language",
"Just Sit There Right Now" by Hafiz translated by Daniel Ladinsky reprinted from
Love Poems from God: Twelve Voices from the East and West, by Daniel Ladinsky
(Penguin) Copyright © 2002. Used with permission of Daniel Ladinsky.
"Keeping Watch" reprinted from *I Heard God Laughing: Poems of Hope and Joy*
by Hafiz and Daniel Ladinsky (Penguin), Copyright © 2006.
Used with permission of Daniel Ladinsky.
"The Risen, Living Christ" reprinted from *Prayer, Fear, and Our Powers: Finding Our
Healing, Release, and Growth in Christ* by Flora Slosson Wuellner. Copyright © 1989.
Used by permission of Upper Room Books.
Poem "There is a contemplative in all of us…" by Alan P. Tory, (b. 1904) is under
copyright control. Reprinted from Northumbria Community's *Celtic Daily Prayer.*
(HarperOne), Copyright © 2002. Used with permission of Northumbria Community.
Unable to locate original publisher.
"Faith" by Patrick Overton, reprinted from *The Leaning Tree* Copyright ©1975.
Used with permission of Patrick Overton.
SoulStream Daily Prayers by Karen Webber, Rob Peterson, Cherie Tetz-Christensen
and Jeff Imbach are used with permission of the writers and SoulStream.
Except when noted, all Scripture quotations are from the Holy Bible,
New International Version Copyright © 2011 by Biblica.

Every person in this book is real. In order to protect their privacy, I have not
always used their given names and may have altered some details.

Cover design by Esther Hizsa
Painting *Night Prayer* by Michael Cook

Library and Archives Canada Cataloguing in Publication

Hizsa, Esther, 1957-, author
Seed cracked open / Esther Hizsa.

ISBN (paperback) 978-1-9991907-0-5

1. Christian life. 2. God (Christianity). I. Title.

Visit *An Everyday Pilgrim* at www.estherhizsa.com

"What's 'whispered in the ear' should always find a way to be 'yelled from the rooftops.'"
—Rob Des Cotes (founder of Imago Dei Communities) in a comment to Esther on her blog.

With deep gratitude, this book is dedicated to
Rob Des Cotes
(1954-2016)
and the Tri-City Imago Dei group.

CONTENTS

INTRODUCTION

WHEN WE PRAY, God is usually silent. This makes relating to our Creator awkward, to say the least. No matter how many books on prayer I read, I continued to cry out, "But what does that look like for me right now?"

God heard my cry and answered by showing me the stories in my life. As I paid attention to them, I learned a lot about God and what God has to say. I learned a lot about myself: that I'm loved more than I can ever hope to imagine.

I began writing down my stories and published *Stories of an Everyday Pilgrim* in 2015.

I'd never written a book before, and my writers' group told me I needed a platform to market it.

"A platform?" I said.

"A website. A blog."

My heart sank. I had no idea how to do that.

"I'll show you, Aunt Esther." My niece Pascale Lemire had launched her website, *Dog Shaming,* and it had gone viral. She'd been interviewed by magazines, was publishing a book with Random House, and *Dog Shaming* calendars would soon be selling at the mall.

I biked to her apartment in Vancouver one afternoon. Within three hours, she set me up and got me started. I launched my blog in the summer of 2013.

Now I had a place on the internet where people could meet me and hear about my book. However, to hold their interest, I needed to keep writing regularly. I began posting a story, reflection or poem every Friday at four pm, and I haven't stopped.

What started as a practical necessity became a spiritual practice. Weekly I'd notice what came to my awareness that seemed significant and write about it. Six years later, I have published over 350 posts.

But that doesn't mean much to my readers who don't follow blogs. They keep asking me when I'll put out another book. Others ask if I would publish the prayer retreat outlines we've used in our Imago Dei group. Well, friends, here they are— seventy-eight posts and five prayer retreat outlines.

The stories I included in *Seed Cracked Open* were written from July 2013 to December 31, 2014. Not long afterward, I came across Hafiz's poem "Seed Cracked Open" and Michael Cook's painting *Night Prayer*. Both the poem and image spoke to me of what God was doing in my life during those years.

In 2012, when I was praying the Ignatian Spiritual Exercises Retreat in Daily Life, I had a strange dream. I dreamed that I was married to three men and struggling to justify this marriage. The meaning soon became clear. I was married to three vocations: pastor, writer and spiritual director. The one I loved the least (being a pastor) demanded so much of me that I had little time for spiritual direction or writing. Yet it was hard to let it go; this was the "husband" that paid the bills and fed my need to be needed.

But a seed was planted during my retreat and two years later it cracked open. At the end of 2014, I was laid off from my job as associate pastor of New Life Community Church. Within a year, I published my first book and welcomed new directees.

Formatting this new collection of stories was not a simple matter of cutting and pasting. With fresh eyes, I reread and edited each piece.

As I did, I listened more deeply to my life. I noticed how often I awakened in the night with anxiety and how much I struggled with being good enough. At times, I was humbled by my own vulnerability and wondered if I should even publish a story. Then I laughed at myself because I already have.

And here's the rub. That's what people have thanked me for the most: my willingness to be vulnerable. It means a lot to know we aren't the only ones that feel the way we do.

If that's all you get from my stories, consider yourself a lucky bum.[1]

---

[1] See page 58

SEED CRACKED OPEN

It used to be
That when I would wake in the morning
I could with confidence say,
"What am 'I' going to
Do?"
That was before the seed
Cracked open.
Now Hafiz is certain:
There are two of us housed
In this body,
Doing the shopping together in the market and
Tickling each other
While fixing the evening's food.
Now when I awake
All the internal instruments play the same music:
"God, what love-mischief can 'We' do
For the world
Today?"
—Hafiz[2]

---

[2] Hafiz (c. 1320-1389), "Seed Cracked Open," *Love Poems from God; Twelve Voices from the East and West* (translated by Daniel Ladinsky).

Summer 2013

IT TAKES A DEAD ALTERNATOR TO RAISE A VILLAGE

MY STOMACH FELT queasy. How was this was going to work out?

We were camping in Washington State when the alternator of our '91 Mazda died. At least that's what Fred suspected after he checked under the hood.

"The kicker is that I have a spare alternator at home," he sighed.

Home was three hundred kilometres away and Winthrop, the nearest town, was thirty. We placed the dead alternator in a bike pannier, put on our biking clothes, and headed south to Winthrop to find a mechanic.

Ten kilometres away we discovered Mazama and its amazing general store with a gas station, locally roasted coffee, ice cream, pottery, organics, freshly baked bread, bike rentals—and a pay phone with a phone book. We called the only garage in Winthrop and found out that the mechanic wouldn't be in until Monday. It was Friday and we needed to be in Canada to meet up with my siblings by Monday. Before Fred hung up, he asked about car rentals. The nearest agency was in Omak, a hundred kilometres east.

"The part won't likely be in until Tuesday," Fred surmised. "A new one could cost a couple of hundred bucks and shipping would double the price. I guess I'll have to hitchhike to Omak, rent a car, and go home and get the spare."

My heart sank. "Maybe someone could bring it down to us?" I suggested.

"Not likely."

"It's worth a try." I swallowed my pride and phoned our daughter.

"Ooh, that would be fun. Call me back in twenty minutes; I need to check a few things," she said.

For twenty minutes I enjoyed the idea of Heidi, Jeremy, and Hadrian joining us for the weekend. But that feeling evaporated when Fred called her back. "That's all right," he said. "We'll manage."

God, I know that you are with us in this. What should we do?

I made more calls, but no one was available to make the drive.

Time was ticking, so I began approaching anyone and everyone who stopped at the store and asked them for a ride to Omak. But no one was going east.

Meanwhile, Fred struck up a conversation with another cyclist. "I've hitch-hiked for years in this area and it's very difficult to get a lift that way," he said. "And if you do, there is no guarantee you would want to ride with the person offering to take you. I'd drive you myself, but I have guests coming from Seattle."

"Maybe someone around here would loan us their car," I said wondering if this fellow might.

The cyclist looked at me hard. "Most people around here keep to themselves. I lived here for two years before someone would loan me their car. You don't have two years." He paused to let that sink in and then continued. "I know who can help you: Liam, the mechanic. He can fix anything. He'll get you on the road in no time. I'll call him," he said.

But he didn't have Liam's number. Nor did the staff inside the store that sees him come in every day for coffee. "No worries," the cyclist said, "I'll bike down to his place. It's just five miles down the road. I'll get him to call you. Stay by the phone."

Half an hour later, I was about to call Heidi back and plead our case when I heard a fellow say, "You must be Fred."

Fred showed Liam the faulty alternator, and Liam called up an auto parts store in Twisp, a town just south of Winthrop.

"They can get the part in tomorrow at nine a.m. It's kind of pricey though," Liam said. "A hundred and twenty bucks."

"And the shipping?" I asked.

"That includes the shipping," he said. "Would you like them to order it?"

"Yes!" we said.

Liam offered to drive us down the next day to pick it up, and he didn't want more than the cost of the gas to do it.

"You've been generous with your time already." I said. "It's OK. We can bike down and get it."

Liam sized up the grey-haired couple he was talking to and looked skeptical.

"Really, it's not that far," I said.

Fred offered to give Liam something for his time, but he wouldn't hear of it. He left us his phone number and instructions about what to do if the car still didn't run with the new alternator.

We biked back to the campsite feeling relieved.

After supper, Shirley and EJ came over from two campsites down. We met them the night before when they needed help getting their thirty-year-old Coleman stove to work. When I heard they planned to hike up Cutthroat Pass, I asked them about the snow levels and wondered if it was still too early in the season to get up to the pass. But they were confident. "We'll come by tomorrow and tell you how things go," Shirley said.

Over a glass of wine, we heard about the hike and their lives. Both women are in their sixties. EJ teaches special education in Hawaii and has travelled extensively. Shirley teaches classes in justice at the University of Western Washington and has recently won a humanitarian award for years of advocating for refugees.

When they heard about our day they said they'd drive us to Twisp to pick up the new alternator.

"We're too tired to go on another hike tomorrow anyway," EJ said.

Was I detecting a theme? God's intentions couldn't have been more obvious.

"That would be great," I said.

The next morning, we got into EJ's old Toyota and shared stories all the way to Twisp and back. Before the women went on their way, we exchanged email addresses and hugs.

Fred installed the new alternator and started the engine. No warning lights. He wiggled a happy dance behind the wheel.

We talked about what happened for the rest of the weekend. "You know, if we'd just stayed calm and thought things through, we could have solved the problem ourselves without needing anyone's help," I said. "But I'm kind of glad we didn't."

"Me, too," Fred replied.

Carry each other's burdens,
and in this way you will fulfill the law of Christ.
—Galatians 6:2

THE DEAD ALTERNATOR SPEAKS

FREDERICK BUECHNER ONCE said that if he were to sum up in a few words the essence of everything he was trying to say both as a novelist and as a preacher, it would be this: Listen to your life.[3]

So I'm listening to my life, particularly for what God might be saying to me in the incident with the alternator.

When that happened I was reading *Living Gently in a Violent World* by Jean Vanier, founder of L'Arche communities, and Stanley Hauerwas, a professor of theological ethics. They made compelling arguments for the importance of creating and maintaining diverse, unhurried, and stable communities where each person feels accepted and celebrated. The outcome of the dead alternator not only illustrated what Vanier and Hauerwas were saying but emphasized the extent to which God goes to create these communities.

A violent world has taught me to value efficiency, economy, and independence above all. If I can solve a problem quickly, cheaply, and without asking anyone for help, I will have "done it right." But that day in Mazama, Jesus seemed to be saying, "Really? And what does that get you? Wouldn't you rather take the time to get to know your neighbour?"

Core members of L'Arche community are developmentally disabled. To join this community you need to be willing to slow down and take two hours to eat a meal with a core member or

---

[3] Frederick Buechner, *Now and Then: A Memoir of Vocation*, 87.

bathe them. Hauerwas dares us to believe that "we have all the time we need to do what needs to be done."[4]

Thus endeth the lesson of the dead alternator.

Or so I thought. A week later it spoke again.

I spent a sleepless night. I had hoped a certain well-known author would consider writing a foreword for my book. But the long silence after the second email said the one word I didn't want to hear. Disappointment hounded me until I remembered all the people that I asked for a ride to Omak. They had all turned me down.

In retrospect, I was glad they did. Their collective "no" spared us from needlessly making the trek home to get the spare alternator and agonizing over how to get a rental car over the border. A "no" can be a good thing, a good gift.

I went to sleep comforted by that thought.

The next day the dead alternator had still more to say to me.

I was biking home from seeing my spiritual director when I ran over a two-inch nail. It went right through the tire and out the sidewall. I turned my bike over and, with a fair bit of effort, pulled out the nail. I replaced the inner tube then biked the remaining twenty-two kilometers back feeling proud of my accomplishment.

When I got home and showed the nail to Fred, he was amazed I made it home with two holes in my tire.

"Good thing we have a spare tire," I said.

That's when we discovered we didn't. In fact, we'd travelled our whole vacation without a spare and my tires are 650s and hard to find.

I was pretty ticked off. "You promised you would always bring a spare tire when we go on bicycling trips. What if this happened when we were on a big ride with my brothers and sister?"

---

[4] Jean Vanier and Stanley Hauerwas, *Living Gently in a Violent World,* 47.

Then I caught myself worshipping the idol of efficiency, economy and independence again. What if that had happened? Would that have been so bad? The dead alternator reminded me that Jesus is with us in every eventuality—and that he often brings a surprise along.

Listen to your life.
See it for the fathomless mystery it is.
In the boredom and pain of it,
no less than in the excitement and gladness:
touch, taste, smell your way to the holy
and hidden heart of it,
because in the last analysis
all moments are key moments,
and life itself is grace.
—Frederick Buechner[5]

---

[5] Frederick Buechner, *Now and Then: A Memoir of Vocation*, 87.

THE FEARFULLY AND WONDERFULLY MADE FARTING MACHINE

TWICE A MONTH on a Saturday our grandchildren, Hadrian and Hannah, have a sleepover at our house. The tried and true routine begins with a trip to the park or pool in the afternoon.

One Saturday we took the five-year-old cousins to an outdoor pool where Hadrian spent most of his time using a water toy to propel water thirty feet in the air. Hadrian loves all things mechanical. He loves elastics, coil door stoppers, and bubble machines.

At bedtime, I read to them with Hannah on one side of me on our queen-sized bed and Hadrian on the other. Halfway through Hannah's selection, *Riverbank Rumpus*, I stopped.

"Hadrian, was that you?"

"P.U.," said Hannah.

"Scuse me," Hadrian said quietly.

While we read the book he chose, a book about trucks, I smelled another one.

"Hadrian, was that you, again?"

"Scuse me," he said again.

The third time it happened, I was reminded of the night his dad went into his bedroom to check on him before turning in. Hadrian was sound asleep, half on, half off his bed. As Jeremy got him comfortably settled, a stinky odor arose followed by a "scuse me" from the boy still asleep.

After two stories from the Jesus Storybook Bible, it was time to tuck them into their beds with kisses and prayers. First

Hannah, then Hadrian. That's when the fourth one silently erupted.

"Hadrian," I said, "you are a farting machine."

Both children laughed hysterically.

"I'm a farting machine," Hadrian said and giggled with delight. "I'm a farting machine!" he repeated with wonder.

I praise you because
I am fearfully and wonderfully made;
your works are wonderful,
I know that full well.
—Psalm 139:14

HIDDEN IN THE CLEFT OF THE ROCK

ONE FRIDAY I misplaced my cell phone.

Fred and I drove to Heidi's place where I thought I'd left it. I was about to go inside to see if I could find it when Fred said, "Look down."

My cell phone was in the gravel behind our car. There was no doubt that we'd just driven over it. I picked it up, wiped off the dust, and tested it out. It still worked!

I couldn't believe it. It must have fallen into a hollow of gravel, so the full weight of the car didn't crush it.

In the days that followed, what happened kept coming to mind, as if God wanted me to notice something about it, as if God was saying something in it.

Monday I attended a prayer retreat and was drawn to Psalm 62. It spoke of God being our refuge and our fortress. At the close of that retreat, I mentioned what happened with my cell phone and a friend said, "It's like you've been placed in the cleft of the rock."

She was referring to Exodus 33 when God hid Moses in the cleft of the rock while God's glory passed by and Song of Songs when the lover finds his beloved in the cleft of the rock and delights to see her face and hear her voice. The image of the cleft in the rock speaks of a God who protects us, delights in us, and cherishes us. That was Monday.

Tuesday I mentioned what happened with my cell phone to my spiritual director. "It reminds me of that Bible verse about God being with us when we pass through deep waters. It's in Isaiah," she said.

"Yes. I think God is telling me: 'Even if you feel like you've been run over by a car, I will be with you. You'll be all right.'"

Thursday morning three scriptures "happened" to be in my daily reading. The first one was Psalm 28:7,

The Lord is my strength and my shield; my heart trusts in God, and God helps me.

The second one was 2 Corinthians 4:16-18,

Therefore we do not lose heart. Though outwardly we are wasting away, yet inwardly we are being renewed day by day. For our light and momentary troubles are achieving for us an eternal glory that far outweighs them all. So we fix our eyes not on what is seen, but on what is unseen, since what is seen is temporary, but what is unseen is eternal.

And the third one was (I'm sure you saw this coming) Isaiah 43:2,

When you pass through the waters, I will be with you; and when you pass through the rivers, they will not sweep over you. When you walk through the fire, you will not be burned; the flames will not set you ablaze.

Do you think God was trying to tell me something?

WHERE DO YOU WANT TO LIVE?

I HAVE NO doubt that God is speaking to me—in the incident with my cell phone, in conversations with friends, and in the scriptures I read. The message is clear: "You are precious to me. I will look after you, no matter what happens. I will be your safe place."

I like what God is saying, but why is God telling me this? What am I about to step into?

As I think about it, I'm drawn to the story of Jesus calming the storm.[6]

The disciples follow Jesus into a boat to cross the Sea of Galilee. Peter, Andrew, James and John are seasoned fishermen living in a culture that historically fears the sea. They know how precarious this crossing can be; they have their superstitions. But Jesus' parables are changing their world view. And his miracles! Jesus healed so many people. If he can do that, he can do anything. With budding confidence, they relax and set sail. Jesus, exhausted from the crowds, falls asleep with his head on a pillow.

Dark clouds appear on the horizon. The wind picks up; waves slap against the hull of the boat. The disciples reef the sail. A few minutes later in the driving rain, they take it down altogether. Waves spill over the gunwale and threaten to swamp the boat. Chilled to the bone, the disciples bail water as fast as they can. But they can't empty the boat of their panic. As

---

[6] Mark 4:35-41

Anthony Bloom put it in *Beginning to Pray*, the storm that is raging around the disciples now rages inside them.[7]

The disciples grab Jesus and shake him. "Master, save us. Don't you care if we drown?"

Jesus wakes up, takes stock of the situation, and looks at them. The disciples read his face: he's not afraid, but he's not happy either. He rebukes them for their lack of faith, then stands up and tells the storm to pipe down.

Then there is "a great calm." The disciples turn to each other and wonder, "Who is this guy?"

What was God saying to the disciples as they listened to their lives that day? What is God saying to me?

Was the point that God is asleep, and when we're in trouble we'd better wake up God or we'll die? If that were true, Jesus would have thanked the disciples instead of scolding them.

If they were just supposed to trust Jesus in everything, why did he calm the storm? Why didn't Jesus just say, "Don't worry, you can trust me. We'll weather this storm together."?

I'm sure there is more than one reason why Jesus calmed the storm—the main one being to answer the question: "Who is this? Even the wind and the waves obey him!" (Answer: God.)

But I begin to see another reason why Jesus did it.

Jesus wanted the disciples to have faith and trust in him. But maybe the disciples had no clue what that kind of trust looks like—or feels like. So Jesus showed them.

In a way, he is saying to us, "See that storm? That's what's in you. See this calm? This is what's in me. Now, where do you want to live?"

> *And he awoke and rebuked the wind and said to the sea,*
> *"Peace! Be still!"*
> *And the wind ceased, and there was a great calm.*
> —Mark 4:3 (ESV)

---

[7] Anthony Bloom, *Beginning to Pray,* 90.

GOD ISN'T ALWAYS TRYING TO TEACH US STUFF

GOD KNOWS OUR thoughts even before we do.[8] And having heard all our thoughts, God must have a lot to say. Could our lives be libraries full of the other half of our conversations with God?

"If God speaks anywhere, it is into our personal lives that God speaks," says Frederick Buechner. "[God] speaks not just through the sounds we hear, of course, but through events in all their complexity and variety, through the harmonies and disharmonies and counterpoint of all that happens... [but] to try to express in even the most insightful and theologically sophisticated terms the meaning of what God speaks through the events of our lives is as precarious a business as to try to express the meaning of the sound of rain on the roof or the spectacle of the setting sun."[9]

When I first began the "precarious business" of deciphering God's messages, I kept listening for what God was trying to teach me. I was sure I was doing something wrong, and that God, ever vigilant, wanted to fix me.

Then, in my spiritual direction training, Steve Imbach shared this story:

"Once when I was travelling, I spent a sleepless night on an uncomfortable bed. In the middle of the night I cried out, 'God,

---

[8] Psalm 139:2,4
[9] Frederick Buechner, *The Sacred Journey*, 1, 3-4.

what are you trying to teach me? I'd like to know, so I can learn it and get back to sleep.' Immediately I heard the inner voice of God reply, 'I'm not trying to teach you anything.' That's when I realized God isn't always trying to teach us stuff."

Imagine a long-term relationship with someone who's only concerned with what they can teach you. There would always be a distance between the two of you, with one feeling burdened and the other inadequate.

Jesus loves us and does express that love by guiding and correcting us, but he is more than a teacher. He is also our friend, our brother, and our husband (since the church is the bride of Christ). So he expresses his love in many ways: by comforting us when troubled, by bringing reconciliation and healing, by helping us find meaning and purpose, and by keeping us company on sleepless nights. He enjoys giving us what we need and hides these gifts out in the open for us to find.

More than anything else, Jesus loves being with us. He keeps telling us that in a God kind of a way—a heart in my cappuccino, a finger-painted sunset, a cancelled appointment that gives me breathing room, or a cell phone that survives being run over by a car.

This is my Father's world.
He shines in all that's fair.
In the rustling grass, I hear him pass.
He speaks to me everywhere.
—Maltbie D. Babcock[10]

---

[10] Maltbie D. Babcock, "This is My Father's World," 1901.

GOD, HOW ARE YOU LOVING ME IN THIS?

BEFORE I PUBLISHED last Friday's post, I emailed Steve Imbach for permission to share his story about the sleepless night. In response, he said, "If it happened now I would probably ask, 'God, how are you loving me in this?'"

When life is difficult, we often ask, "God, where are you?" (assuming God is absent) or "What am I doing wrong?" (assuming God is punishing us). But when we are recall how good, compassionate and attentive God is, we can ask, "God, how are you loving me in this?"

I recently had a conversation with someone and could tell by their body language that they were hurt or angry with me. That caused me to have a sleepless night.

I told myself to stop being so sensitive and not to worry about it. I tried distracting myself but when that didn't work, I tried to figure out how I could fix the situation that caused the uncomfortable feelings in the first place. I asked God, "What did I do wrong?"

For days afterward, I was convinced that the only thing Jesus wanted to tell me was that I should think before I speak and be more considerate. But Jesus wasn't interested in giving me a report card.

During a silent retreat, God whispered, "Ask me how I am loving you in this."

My Abba reminded me of the cell phone, the cleft in the rock, and the story of how Jesus calmed the storm, and how they spoke of God's maternal and secure love for me.

Then, God asked me a question, "What are you afraid of?"

In the silence, I recalled how badly I felt about that disturbing conversation. Suddenly I knew what I was afraid of and why.

When I was a child, I could be picked on for any number of reasons. I always wanted to know what I was doing wrong, so I didn't do it again. If I could do things right, then I would be safe and people would stop hurting me.

In God's great calm I saw it as plain as day: I'm afraid of doing things wrong. I think I have to get things right to be safe.

Jesus wanted me to notice all this so I could envision another way to live. He was inviting me into a new reality where I don't have to get things right to be safe.

"I'll be your safe place, your rock and fortress." Jesus keeps saying, "And every time you see the scratches on your cell phone, I'll remind you of that."

God, the one and only—
I'll wait as long as you say.
Everything I need comes from you,
so why not?
You're the solid rock under my feet,
breathing room for my soul,
An impregnable castle:
I'm set for life.
—Psalm 62:1, 2 (The Message, adapted)

WHAT JESUS CARES ABOUT

WALKING HOME FROM the store I run into "Philip," a guy in the neighbourhood who attends our church once in a while. He smiles and says hello, but frowns when I ask him how he's doing.

He tells me, as he does every time I see him, about his visits to the doctor, the constant pain, the cut in support funding, and the struggle to make ends meet. I encourage him again to go to the church for prayer on Tuesday nights. He describes again the websites that stop him from going to church. According to them, most churches have been doing it all wrong. "I get so confused," he says, "I don't know what to do."

We talk for a while, and then I say, "Don't worry about figuring it all out. That's not what Jesus cares about. What he really cares about is you and hanging out with you."

Afterward, I feel bad for trying to fix Philip instead of listening more deeply. Lord, please help Philip. And help me be a better listener.

The next morning I sit down to pray and recall my Grade 5 teacher, Mrs Sidon. She was old (at least fifty) and stocky with short, tight curly grey hair and round wire-framed glasses. She wore plain dark dresses and orthopedic shoes and liked to hold the wooden pointer when she taught. She was so strict that everyone dreaded going into Grade 5.

But I liked Mrs Sidon. She was kind to me.

Whenever I was bullied or teased at school, I would cry and run to the teacher. One lunch hour, I was upset about something and found Mrs Sidon in our empty classroom. She wiped my tears with her handkerchief and looked me in the eyes. "Ten-year-olds aren't supposed to cry so much," she said. So I stopped.

Mrs Sidon didn't ask me why I cried so much. I wonder what life would be like if she had. But she didn't ask questions like that. She didn't have that to give. Instead, she gave me what she did have: a valuable tool that helped me survive elementary school.

I sense an inner prompting to thank God for her, and I do.

I enjoy the feeling of gratitude for a moment until regret about how I spoke to Philip pushes it aside. That's when I hear Jesus thank me for giving Philip a valuable tool to survive. "It's what you had in you at the time, and it was enough," Jesus says to me, "Thank you."

Boundless gratitude is my soul's response.

O my Beloved,
You have searched me and known me...
You encompass me with love where'er I go,
and Your strength is my shield.
Such sensitivity is too wonderful for me;
It is high; boundless gratitude is my soul's response.
—Psalm 139:1, 6[11]

---

[11] Nan C. Merrill, *Psalms For Praying: An Invitation to Wholeness*

SETTLING ACCOUNTS
WITH MY FEARS

I BITE MY lip. Did I say too much? Push too hard? Why did she hang up so suddenly? In our conversation, I took a risk and challenged my friend's perspective; now I fear the worst. I'm afraid she'll stop talking to me. I feel powerless. It weighs on me while I go for a bike ride with Fred.

Anxiety prompts me to keep returning to my inner fortress and pray, "Help. Please."

The phone rings when we get home. It's my friend. She explains why she had to end the call so abruptly and says she'll think about what I said. I breathe out a "Thank You" after I hang up the phone.

I enjoy the relief for a while until another fear takes its place! I picture a whole queue of fears extending around velvet ropes and stanchions like a line up at the bank. The fears fidget and sigh as each one waits for its turn to make deposits and withdrawals. Sheesh! Will this ever end?

The fear staring at me now reminds me that in a week I'm leading our monthly prayer retreat. "What's your scripture? What's your plan?" it demands to know. The questions send ripples of tension across my shoulders and down my arms.

Once again I return to my fortress and pray, "Help. Please."

I don't like these fears; I'd like to close my wicket and be rid of the lot of them.

"O that you would vanquish my fears, Beloved," writes Nan C. Merrill in her paraphrase of Psalm 139.[12] But then she goes on to say, "Yet are these not the very thorns that focus my thoughts upon you?"

I may be discouraged by the long line up of fears, but Jesus isn't. He knows they serve a purpose: they bring me back to him.

I hope one day I won't need them or at least need fewer of them. I suspect that when my fears have nothing useful left to offer, Jesus will gladly close their accounts.

O that You would vanquish my fears, Beloved;
O that ignorance and suffering would depart from me—
My ego separates me from true abandonment,
to surrendering myself into your Hands!
Yet are these not the very thorns
that focus my thoughts upon You?
Will I always need reminders
to turn my face to You?
I yearn to come to You in love,
to learn of your mercy and wisdom!
—Psalm 139:19-22[13]

---

[12] Nan C. Merrill, *Psalms For Praying: An Invitation to Wholeness*
[13] Ibid.

IN THIS PRECISE LOCATION

I'M INTO THE second week of my cold with little energy to do more than watch *Big Bang Theory*. I borrowed Season Three from the library and put my feet up. In one episode a guest is invited to Leonard and Sheldon's apartment. She is about to sit down in the vacant spot on the couch when Howard, Raj, and Leonard gasp in unison. "You can't sit there! That's where Sheldon sits."

"Can't he sit somewhere else?" the newbie asks as if this were a reasonable possibility. Before Sheldon can explain, Penny, the girl next door who is generally irritated with the obsessively compulsive genius, recites—word for word—Sheldon's rationale for needing to sit in that precise location. Sheldon is delighted: Penny understands him.

It's a touching scene and a welcome interlude from my current reality. My cold is getting me down. I'm bothered by things I've said and done and regret the inconveniences I've caused others. When I record them in my journal I realize they're rather minor. The offended will survive. I bet my transgressions are no longer on anyone's mind but mine. That doesn't comfort me though. If such little things bother me, I know I'm not doing very well.

I've felt this way before. It will pass. But in the meantime, I wish I weren't in this overly sensitive place again. I think of all the reasons why I landed in this precise location: not enough prayer or exercise top the list.

I tell God how disappointed I am in myself. And what do I hear in response?

God simply says, "I know."

Just like Penny, God doesn't blame but simply understands.

Unlike Penny, God can maintain that compassion for a whole episode.

But you, Lord, are a compassionate and gracious God,
slow to anger, abounding in love and faithfulness.
—Psalm 86:15

PRAYING IN THE CRACKS

I WENT TO my first spiritual director a dozen years ago while I was studying at Regent College.

After a few sessions, my director said gently, "You have a lot of noisy, discouraging tapes playing in your head. I can't compete with them."

I swallowed hard. "What can I do?"

"Do you pray?" she asked.

"Yes. Sometimes. Not as much as I'd like."

"How about praying in the cracks?"

"The what?"

"The cracks. The spaces that naturally occur in your day as you walk from one class to another, as you stand in line at the grocery store, or wait for an elevator. In those spare moments, instead of thinking about what you need to do next or trying to solve problems, just allow God to love you."

"That's it?"

"Yes. Do you think you can do that?"

"I think so."

"Trust me. If you pray in the cracks, it will change your life."

As I walked from her office to the bus stop, I decided to try it. I began to pray and all kinds of thoughts flooded into my mind: things I should pray for, things I should do. Then I looked down at a crack in the sidewalk and stopped. Just allow God to love you, she had said.

Red and golden leaves caught my eye. Dry brown ones crunched underfoot. I listened to the birds and thought about being God's beloved child.

After that, whenever I found myself waiting for anything (and remembered to pray), I quieted my heart and imagined God saying to me, "You are my beloved child. With you, I am well pleased."

In those cracks, God deposited seeds of Christ's kingdom. Before long, I found myself relaxing in the shade of a mustard tree with more freedom to pray and enjoy God's presence.

A dozen years later I still pray in the cracks. And those old tapes? They're not as loud as they used to be.

Surely goodness and mercy will follow me
all the days of my life;
and I shall dwell in the heart of the Beloved
forever. Amen.
—Psalm 23:6[14]

---

[14] Nan C. Merrill, *Psalms For Praying: An Invitation to Wholeness*

WILL I OPEN MY HEART TO GOD?

EVERY MORNING, ALONG with others in our dispersed SoulStream community, I say this prayer.

Blessed Trinity,
I receive your love, your presence and this day as a gift from you.
I open my heart to you.
Please lead me deeper into your transforming love
as we live these next hours together.
Amen.[15]

The first sentence tells us what God does. All Three Persons of the Trinity love us, remain with us, and give us each day.

The second line, the line I most often forget to say, reminds me of what I must do: open my heart to God. But will I do it?

I picture myself opening up my heart. Inside is my life, not as I'd like it to be, but as it is. I feel anxious; like I did that day the minister came to visit and asked to use the washroom. The main one was occupied and before I could stop Fred, he ushered the reverend into our bedroom and showed him to the ensuite bathroom—the only two rooms I hadn't cleaned.

Opening our hearts to receive anyone's presence is risky. Inevitably they will find our grimy edges and be tempted to judge us. Sometimes they do.

---

[15] Karen Webber, SoulStream Community's Morning Prayer

It takes courage to let Jesus wander around your house. But when I'm brave enough to invite him in, I'm often surprised by what he notices and how he responds.

Take, for example, the time I had an argument with someone. It was days before I could meet Jesus at the door and look him in the eye. He noticed my apprehension and said softly, "I know why you've been avoiding me. You think I'll take his side."

I knew it was true. I sat with that thought in the spacious silence until the din of fear receded, and it was quiet enough to hear God's heart.

I asked Jesus what he saw.

The Holy Spirit stirred in my belly, sending a warmth into my chest. My shoulders and arms relaxed. I felt how important it was to God that I had spoken up for myself and had been heard. I knew it without a doubt.

As I sat longer with Jesus, I also understood what the other person was trying to say and why he was angry. My heart softened toward him.

In the last line of the prayer, I ask the Triune God, "Lead me deeper into your transforming love as we (God and all those in my world) live these next hours together."

That's exactly what God was doing.

ALL SHE WANTS IS A DOOR

"YOU KNOW WHAT'S making me mad right now? I'll tell you," Paul[16] said looking me in the eye. We were standing outside the entrance to the Greenhouse, a renovated house on New Life Church's property, waiting for the soup to heat up.

Every Wednesday, volunteers come here to offer people who are homeless or at risk of homelessness a place to gather for conversation, coffee, and a bowl or two of soup. We call it the Wednesday Lunch Club.

Paul, one of the regulars, put out his cigarette and told me what angered him. "I know this woman who was into hard drugs, bad stuff. She got clean and she's been clean for a year or so. She's about thirty-five, not unattractive," he said. "But here's the thing: she can't find a place to live. She's got the money, but every time she calls about an apartment, as soon as they hear she's on welfare, click." He imitated someone hanging up the phone. "So what does she do? She stays where she can, on people's couches. And Esther, some of those people aren't nice. Way too often in the middle of the night, if a man lives there, he will wake her up and take advantage of her."

Paul stepped closer to the open door and grabbed the doorknob. "All she wants is this. All she wants is a door that she can close and lock and feel safe on the other side."

I kept thinking about what Paul said and talked about it over dinner with Fred. "It's just not right. Something's got to be done.

---

[16] Not his real name

Wanda Mulholland and all the people on the Burnaby Task Force on Homelessness have spent countless hours talking to officials and raising awareness about homelessness. And still, there isn't a homeless shelter in Burnaby[17]—let alone housing for people like this woman."

Fred shook his head. "And I keep hearing on the radio how much money government departments have spent with nothing to show for it."

"We could give more money, but we can never give enough to house the people who need it," I said. "We have to do something more. We need to pray."

"Alas, has it come to that?" someone once said when faced with a similar dilemma, as if resorting to prayer meant there was no hope.

"We need someone big and powerful to make big and powerful changes in our city, so why not talk to the God of the universe?" I said.

So I speak to God often about the need for more doors and homes. I pray that I will see what Jesus is doing and join him in his work of bringing good news to the poor and setting the oppressed free. I thank God that this woman has a friend like Paul.

"The Spirit of the Lord is on me,
because he has anointed me
to proclaim good news to the poor.
God has sent me to proclaim freedom for the prisoners
and recovery of sight for the blind,
to set the oppressed free,
to proclaim the year of the Lord's favor."
—Luke 4:18

---

[17] Burnaby finally built and opened a permanent shelter in 2019.

FEEDING A FRAGILE DESIRE

I GUESS IT'S time, I thought as I biked along. In my spirit, I knew I was ready to face my shame about overeating.

I meet with Karen, my spiritual director, regularly. The sacred space we share allows me to get a sense of what God is doing in my life. Over the years, I've talked with her about a number of things. But the one topic I managed to avoid until now is my attachment to food.

"I know I shouldn't eat so much, but when it comes right down to it, I like eating. It's pleasurable and gives me comfort. Relaxing with a snack and a book is my reward for a hard day's work," I told Karen. "But I'm gaining weight and my clothes don't fit. My cholesterol is too high and the doctor said weight is a factor. And overeating is unethical. Why should I eat more than I need? I have all these good reasons not to overeat, but it doesn't stop me from doing it."

"What do you long for?" Karen asked.

"I want to be freed from this compulsion. I know it doesn't glorify God, but that doesn't seem to matter. I just turn my back on God and eat anyway." Tears came as I spoke. "Every time I overeat, I feel my heart hardening. I wish I had a softer heart."

"Is there an image that would represent that desire for a soft heart?"

I closed my eyes and waited. After a while, I opened them and said, "I can't picture the desire. All I know is that it's fragile, and Jesus is holding it with me."

"A fragile desire that Jesus is holding with you," she said and nodded. "How does that feel to you?"

"I like that Jesus is with me. That I'm not alone in the struggle. It reminds me of the quote by Richard Rohr, 'God looks for the places in us that are trying to say yes.'"

I was about to grasp onto hope when it dissipated. I teared up again. "These are all nice thoughts, but my desire for food is so much bigger than my desire for God. I'm afraid it will be crushed."

"Is there a prayer you could pray for this fragile desire?"

Then I saw it. Not right away. First, the words came and then the image. I pictured Jesus holding a baby bird in our open hands. It was cheeping away, wanting to be fed. That vulnerable little bird represented my desire to love God more than anything else.

"I could ask the Holy Spirit to feed my desire for God so it grows bigger than any other," I said.

Karen smiled with wonder.

"Every morning when I pray 'I open my heart to you,' I can picture that little bird in our open hands and ask God to increase my desire for him," I said with renewed hope.

I could do that.

As I rode home, I asked God to increase my fragile desire. Many times a day I ask this and, as I do, I picture God feeding me love.

For we know how dearly God loves us,
and we feel this warm love everywhere within us
because God has given us the Holy Spirit
to fill our hearts with God's love.
—Romans 5:5b (The Living Bible)

Advent 1 2013

GETTING READY TO CELEBRATE CHRIST'S BIRTH

IN TWO DAYS, Advent begins and with it comes that stress-inducing question: Are you ready for Christmas? Those words produce a flurry of images—shopping, decorating, baking, Christmas cards, and list making—that sends chills of expectations through my soul. I'm overwhelmed before I begin. How will I ever do it all?

So I've decided that when anyone asks me that question, no matter what I've done or haven't done, I'm going to say "YES!" Because I *am* ready to celebrate Christ's birth.

AN ADVENT PRAYER

Jesus, I am ready.

I'm ready to meet you daily . . .
    reflect on your birth,
    and notice how your story impacts mine.

I'm ready to be silent . . .
    and let myself adore you.

I'm ready to wonder.
    How would you like to be celebrated?
    What gifts shall we give?

I'm ready to let go . . .
    of things on my list that aren't on yours.

I'm ready to gather with others . . .
    to sing, worship, and celebrate.

I'm ready to welcome and receive . . .
    all of who you are
    and all of who I am.

And that means

I'm ready to do all these things
    the only way I can—
    imperfectly and inconsistently.

Come, thou long-expected Jesus.
Come now.
Don't wait until I'm ready.

Come, Thou long-expected Jesus,
Born to set Thy people free;
From our fears and sins release us,
Let us find our rest in Thee.
—Charles Wesley[18]

---

[18] Charles Wesley, "Come, Thou Long-Expected Jesus," 1745.

Advent II 2013

A MYSTERIOUS PLACE OF MEETING

I SPEND THREE days on Bowen Island walking, praying, and watching the seagulls. I notice that when one or two birds land on the calm sea others follow. God seems to be telling me that as I rest in Love, others will be drawn to that rest as well.

I love this peaceful, attractive image and carry it home.

On the ferry ride back, every noise is amplified. The ship's horn signals the return of Real Life. I join the queue and disembark into a crowd of tense faces, deadlines, emails, phone messages, disappointments and complications.

The next two days offer no solitude. I notice that I'm irritable and judgmental. People squawk and fly off.

Two o'clock in the morning, I'm awake. Tired of tossing and turning, I get up and try to pray and write this mood out of me. My own words land and flick cold wet thoughts:

> *I'm ready to welcome and receive . . .*
> *all of who you are*
> *and all of who I am.*

No, I'm not. I don't like all of who I am. I don't like being irritable or unkind. I want to be that gentle bird floating peacefully, attractively.

Rob Des Cotes, founder of Imago Dei communities, once said that our weaknesses endear us to God.

He quoted Johannes B. Metz. "Only through poverty of spirit do we draw near to God; only through it does God draw near to us. Poverty of spirit is the meeting point of heaven and earth, the mysterious place where God and we encounter each other."

When I first heard that quote, I couldn't quite picture "poverty of spirit." Now, I not only see it, I feel its salty chill.

Sometimes I have the grace to be still and speak out of God's silence the words that draw others to God.

And sometimes I'm just another scrappy gull in a restless flock.

But the Spirit reminds me that God loves all of who I am all the time. Jesus not only meets me in my contented stillness but mysteriously descends into my soul's stable and makes his home there.

Blessed are the poor in spirit,
for theirs is the kingdom of heaven.
—Matthew 5:3.

Advent III 2013

INCARNATION: SOME ASSEMBLY REQUIRED

I open my door
to welcome all that You are
and
    everyone comes in

anxious
thoughtful
joyous
distraught
expectant
ANGRY
    (with compassion crushing
    blame baring
    vulnerability)
lost

God unassembled

I feel
Your need
to be
    us

OUR DARKEST HOUR

TOMORROW IS THE first day of summer in the southern hemisphere. But for those of us on the other side of the world, winter begins with the longest night of the year. Advent comes to a climax in our darkest hour.

I began the Advent season with a confidence that has been repeatedly derailed. (I must confess I haven't yet said YES in capital letters to anyone that asked me if I'm ready for Christmas.) I was ready for moments of wonder and joy—and they have come—but I have also been tripped by feelings of inadequacy and am tempted to just get through this season. I look around and see others struggling for more light too. These dark days make me increasingly aware of how broken we all are and how desperately we need God.

Desperation prepares our hearts like nothing else.

Two weeks ago, I was having a bowl of soup with "Tom" who has been homeless since spring. Before I could sit down he wanted a hug. In the three years I've known this man, he's never asked me for a hug.

"I was arrested," he said, "for no good reason. The cops held me for twelve hours. When I asked for my stuff back they said they were keeping it… for evidence."

"What?"

"They took everything I owned. I managed to get another backpack and sleeping bag from Progressive Housing and someone gave me these pants, but they were made for a f***ing midget."

He finished his soup and left before I could find words to comfort him.

In a staff meeting that afternoon, we prayed for Tom, but I kept imagining him irritated by Christmas carols, frustrated with an empty-handed God.

Tom returned the following Wednesday. "Look at me," he said grinning and showing off his fur-lined coat.

"What happened?"

"Things went from bad to worse, and I didn't know what to do. I had nothing. Finally, I cried out to God, 'I need clothes. And I know you can provide them.' Within five minutes I found this! I'm not kidding, five minutes later I received this coat and these clothes." He held open his coat so I could see his new shirt, jeans and shoes.

He went on. "I never believed God loved me, but I now know it. I know he loves me," he said and began to weep. "These are not tears of sadness, but tears of joy. I'm the prodigal son come home. God put a robe around me and shoes on my feet."

The true light, which enlightens everyone, was coming into the world.
The light shines in the darkness,
and the darkness did not overcome it.
—John 1:9, 5

Christmas 2013

A PROBLEM OF ORIENTATION AND PROXIMITY

TODAY WE CELEBRATE good news of great joy that is for all people: God has come to earth to save us. But what has Jesus come to save us from? The very thing that has robbed us of life: sin. The angels' announcement was good news for all people because all of us have sinned and fallen short of what God intended for us.

During the Advent season, as the days got shorter and the nights longer, I became acutely aware of the painful effects of sin—mine and everyone else's. I suspected the Holy Spirit was getting me ready to receive the One who came to address it.

When I have been sinned against, I welcome such a saviour. I'm glad Jesus has come to rectify the injustice I've suffered. I want him to defend me and address those who have wronged me.

But what happens when I'm the sinner? The news that Jesus has come to address my sin doesn't sound good, nor does it fill me with great joy. No one likes to be found guilty. The angels knew that, yet they beckoned us all to rejoice. They wanted everyone to celebrate because Jesus did not come to condemn and reject us, but to inform and return us to God. For what is sin but a turning away from Love?

All of us have, at one time or another, turned away from God and tried to get what we want from others. But they cannot meet all our needs. And so, on some level, they felt violated because, in fact, they have been.

I have come to realize that sin indicates a problem of orientation and proximity. When I turn away from God and move further from Love to seek security, significance, and empowerment from others, I will inevitably cause suffering.

God's solution to all this violence was to send Jesus to redirect us to Love. When I turn toward Jesus, his love draws me closer and I begin to experience God's loving attentiveness, power, and provision. I can ask for what I need and, as I wait on God to provide it, I become rightly related to others.

"Come and follow me," Jesus said to his disciples.[19] When they weren't sure they could trust him, he said, "Come and see."[20] When they got confused and lost their way, he found them— crying in the garden, disappointed on the road, guilty by the shore—and led them back to God.

On Christmas, we celebrate God's gift of a saviour. Jesus has come to find us and bring us home.

That is good news.

'Rejoice with me, for I have found my sheep that was lost.'
—Luke 15:6

---

[19] Matthew 4:19
[20] John 1:39

WHAT IF MARY HAD SAID, "NO"?

THE ANGEL GABRIEL appeared to Mary and told her she had found favour with God and was going to give birth to God's son. Mary wondered how this could possibly be true since she was a virgin. Yet she responded with the words, "I am the Lord's servant, may it be to me as you have said."[21]

Her immortal "Yes" has been painted, written about, and celebrated ever since. But what if Mary had said, "No." What if, at that moment, she pulled the plug on the most beautiful aria in history? Imagine the pained look on Gabriel's face if he had to tell the hosts of heaven to pack up shop. Would that have been the end of the story or would they have hastily gone looking for another young woman to take Mary's place?

But Gabriel did not come to ask Mary if she wanted to bear the Son of God. He simply announced what was going to happen: the Holy Spirit would come upon her, the power of the Most High overshadow her, and the One born to her would be called Jesus.

It seems to me that if Mary didn't want to hear Gabriel's news and told him to go away, she still would have gotten pregnant and given birth to our Lord. But Jesus would have been born to a mother who didn't want him, didn't love him, and would not have encouraged him to be himself. He would have grown up to do all that God asked him to while bearing the sorrow of being rejected by his own mother. Isaiah 49:15 would have become prophetic: "Can a mother forget the baby at her

---

[21] Luke 1:38

breast and have no compassion on the child she has borne? Though she may forget, I will not forget you."

If Mary had interpreted Gabriel's message as a burden foisted upon her, she would have gone down in history as the woman who missed the opportunity to enjoy mothering the Saviour of the world.

Mary's story pierces our hearts because we too have been presented with a great opportunity. Whether we choose it or not, we have been overshadowed by the Holy Spirit who finds one way or another to be born in us. Everything in life has the potential of opening us to God. God uses these things to enter the core of our being, so God can love us and be loved by us. The Holy comes to us... whether or not we see it.

The question is not: will I allow God's kingdom to come— for it most surely will—but, will I, like Mary, believe I have found favour in his sight? Will I embrace this holy gift?

How silently, how silently,
the wondrous Gift is given!
So God imparts to human hearts
the blessings of His heaven.
No ear may hear His coming,
but in this world of sin,
where meek souls will receive Him still,
the dear Christ enters in.
— Phillips Brooks[22]

---

22 Phillips Brooks, "O Little Town of Bethlehem," 1868.

Winter 2014

FREE AS A BIRD

IT'S JANUARY. THE New Year brings me closer to spring and the possibility of more emotional energy. Dark December is a hard month for me. I keep praying that my desire for God will increase, but other desires trap me, and I feel somewhat numb and lost. I gripe at God. "Just tell me what you want me to do to get out of this place."

I think of people I know who struggle with long-term illnesses. They too long to be free as a bird—as free as the swallow that my son-in-law, Jeremy, saw while he was in hospital for the nth time because of Crohn's disease. His song Swallow[23] speaks of my desire to be free.

Swallow,
fly to your home
in the wall of the hospital.
I am stuck here inside,
and you may be,
but I'm not free at all.

My dance partner has been
this intravenous pole.
I am tired of the spin;
I am so tired of spinning her.

---

[23] Jeremy Braacx, (Geometric Shapes)"Swallow", *View from My Hospital Bed.*

Swallow,
fly to your home
in the wall of the hospital.
I am stuck here inside,
and you may be,
but I'm not free at all.

My mind's been going whirr-tick-tick
to the sound of my IV pump.
I have been so tired and sick,
so sick and tired of thinking about—

Swallow,
fly to your home
in the wall of the hospital.
I am stuck here inside,
and you may be,
but I'm not free at all.

Swallow, fly into my chest.
Make a nest; build a home.
Swallow, fly into my chest.
Make a nest; fill the hole
in my soul.

I heard of one who can raise the dead.
Transform the view from my hospital bed.

In the silence, as I wait for God to transform my view, a deeper desire rises. *The Cloud of Unknowing* describes it as "a naked intent toward God in the depths of my being." Its flame fills my chest with a sharp longing—not to flee this hole in my soul—but to fill it with God and God's "unending miracle of love."[24]

Words come from a softer place now. "Lord, deepen my love for you."

I find God's reply in the wise words of the fourteenth-century mystic who wrote *The Cloud of Unknowing*: "Though this loving desire is certainly God's gift, it is up to you to nurture it... fix your love on God... Close the doors and windows of your spirit against the onslaught of pests and foes and prayerfully seek God's strength; for if you do so, God will keep you safe from them. Press on then... Our Lord is always ready. Love awaits only your co-operation."[25]

Love,
fly into my chest,
build a nest,
make a home
in my soul.

Help me press on.
Close the door of my heart
to all competing desires
so I do not love anything
more than you.

Amen

---

[24] *The Cloud of Unknowing*, 14th C. anonymous English author, (edited by William Johnston), 50.
[25] Ibid, 47.

NOT AGAIN!

I WENT FOR a walk with a friend the other day. After we greeted each other with a hug, she clipped a microphone on my collar. This silver bullet-shaped microphone transmits my voice to her hearing aids, so she can hear me while we walk.

We soon became engrossed in conversation. When we neared the end of our walk, I noticed the microphone was gone. We prayed and retraced our steps looking for it. We even asked sympathetic passers-by to keep an eye out for it. Eventually, we gave up and said goodbye.

Before getting into the car to go home, I unfastened the coat I had tied around my waist when I got overheated. That's when I found the microphone still clipped to my coat collar. It had been there the whole time!

At this point, you might expect me to mention how God is always with us, even when we are unaware of it or talk about the importance of mindfulness. But really, considering my age, I'd rather just laugh about it. In situations like these, I find myself echoing my grandson, Hadrian. He often says, with a laughing groan, "Not again!"

We have to laugh at ourselves sometimes, and I rarely find myself short of material to laugh about.

The other day I was racing out the door to Scrabble night with friends when I remembered my cell phone needed charging. I grabbed the cord and intended to recharge my phone while we played.

I didn't think of it again until I got home and couldn't find the cord. I looked for it in my backpack and my coat pockets three times with no luck. I emailed my friends; they hadn't seen it either. The next morning I checked the most likely places again and even looked in a coat pocket that I rarely use. As I did I felt a hard object in the sleeve: the plug of the charging cord. Ha! The night before, I had the cord in my hand when I put on my jacket. The cord was still dangling in my sleeve!

When I told my friends what happened, they had a good laugh. And I hope you do too.

Each time the Lord said,
"My grace is all you need.
My power works best in weakness."
—2 Corinthians 12:9 (NLT)

IMMERSED
IN AN OCEAN OF LOVE

I AWAKE WITH an emotional heaviness at four a.m. and remember what caused this feeling. I got hoodwinked by fear in a legitimate disguise: I saw an injustice and pushed the panic button—again. I ended up making a fuss over nothing, and now I wonder if those involved are getting frustrated with me.

I hate these holes in my bucket.

"If you were a leaky bucket and wanted to be filled with God's love," I heard Rob Des Cotes say at a prayer retreat not long ago, "you could either spend your life patching the holes or simply immerse yourself in the ocean of God's love."

When I heard Rob's words, I imagined myself as a bucket, filled and surrounded with love. A deep "ah" relaxed my body.

God is loving me now at four in the morning. God doesn't despise my weaknesses but sees these holes as openings through which I can be filled with love.

I breathe in and out and picture myself lying in God's ocean of love. I hear the pebbles move, feel them shift under me as the cool water flows out and rushes in again. Salty waves flood my weaknesses and recede leaving every filament of their tattered edges as wet and vibrant as anemones.

In the light of day, my fears will have drifted off to sea; I will laugh at myself and wonder why I was so worried. Even if my peers are wearied of me, I will not be undone. God is with me.

But here, now in the night, I don't want a strategy for how to live with my weaknesses. Here and now, I just want to lie in the ocean of God's love and feel God's tireless, boundless love wash in and out of the holes in my soul.

When I awake, I am still with you.
—Psalm 139:18b

WHAT'S A BUCKET TO DO?

I KEEP THINKING of myself as that leaky bucket. I marvel at the fact that I don't need to put myself into God's ocean of love; I'm already there.

The first illusion I had, which I talked about last week, is that I need to fix my holes to be useful to God. The second is that I could ever be empty of God.

When I open myself to God, I do not let in more of God. I am already full of God. Instead, I open myself to the reality that I am in God.

When Darrell Johnson taught at Regent College, he once said in a sermon on John 17, "We are in God and God is in us," then added with a wondrous sigh, "and you can't get much closer than in."

Jesus prayed that we would be one with the Father in the same way he is. God answered that prayer through Jesus' death and resurrection. Yet we keep living as if nothing has changed. Father Thomas Keating, a Benedictine monk, said, "The chief thing that separates us from God is the thought that we are separated from Him. If we get rid of that thought, our troubles will be greatly reduced."[26]

Yes. "That thought" makes me thrash about, frantically trying to keep myself afloat. Jesus smiles. "Let yourself sink into my love. Abide in me and I will bear fruit in you."[27]

---

[26] Thomas Keating, *Open Mind, Open Heart*, 44.
[27] John 15:1-17

I imagine myself again as that leaky bucket sinking into God's ocean of love, not fixing or accomplishing or becoming anything. I feel peaceful.

But it doesn't take long before my ego asks, "So, what are you doing here?"

The answer comes to me in the middle of the night: I am "doing" the will of God. As I rest in God's love, I am fulfilling all God wants me to do with my life in this moment.

In this resting, in God's fullness, I am able to consent to God's loving action in my life. My ego can relax: God is my saviour, sanctifier and guide.

Here in God's ocean of love, with my ego asleep beside me, I am free to enjoy loving God.

God wants nothing more than our consent to be loved.
—Father Thomas Keating

TRAPPED

FRUSTRATED, STUCK, TRAPPED. That's how I felt. That's what I recorded in my account of a spiritual direction session.

I had directed the session and was reflecting on it with other spiritual directors when we gathered for peer supervision. In supervision, we don't focus on the directee and what is going on with them. We focus on the director and what the Holy Spirit is doing in us. We pay special attention to the emotions we experienced as we listened to God and the directee in that sacred space.

My wise and compassionate friends listened carefully to what I'd said and the feelings I experienced during the session. They asked me to say more about them.

"I felt trapped because I didn't know what to do," I said. "When I calmly look back on the situation, I know now what I could have said or asked. But in my panic, I couldn't see those options."

I had experienced the same panicky feeling a few times recently: when I overreacted to a comment, when I tried to call Fred and his cell phone was off, and when I drove back and forth trying to find a house in the dark.

Tears came. "This happens a lot."

"Do you think you're triggered by something in your childhood?" one spiritual director asked.

I thought for a moment, but nothing specific came to mind.

Two days later, in the middle of the night, I remembered a time when I was a young child and my siblings played a prank on me. We were in the curing room of my father's cheese factory. They went out and shut the door, leaving me inside in the dark. They must have assumed I knew how to open the heavy industrial door, but I didn't. It seemed like forever until they came to let me out.

Now, with the help of my friends, I understood how the incident still affected me. I saw a pattern: something happens that I can't control; I feel powerless; my upper body tightens. I have to get out.

When I was in my spiritual direction training, I talked about this childhood memory in a "real play" with another student. I was the directee and he was the spiritual director. He invited me to picture Jesus in the curing room with me. I closed my eyes and saw myself as a little girl. Jesus pulled me onto his lap and enfolded me in his arms. He lit a light in the darkness and smiled.[28]

Jesus is with me when I'm afraid. This truth may not keep me from feeling trapped by life's events. But now, when I sense my upper body tighten, I can think of Jesus' arms around me again and be comforted. Eventually, my eyes will adjust to the dark and will see the options before me.

I will find the open door.

Even the darkness is not dark to you;
the night is as bright as the day
—Psalm 139:12 (NRSV)

---

[28] I wrote about this in "God in the Dark: Theory" in *Stories of an Everyday Pilgrim*, 38.

LUCKY BUMS

"LUCKY BUMS!"

That's how theologian Karl Barth described the poor in spirit who inherit God's kingdom. [29] Ever since someone mentioned that in our Imago Dei group, we have the urge to call each other "lucky bums." It reminds us that we are blessed because of our weaknesses, not in spite of them.

It's hard to resist our culture's compulsion to distance ourselves from our shortcomings or treat them as problems we must overcome or fix. Most of us spend our lives trying to correct our inadequacies and assume this practice pleases God. We envision the model Christian as one who goes "from strength to strength."[30] Communion liturgies praise the Lamb who heals the weakness of our soul, and we presume our frailties are abhorrent to God.

But they are not.

"Our weaknesses endear us to God," said Rob Des Cotes, founder of Imago Dei Communities. The Good Shepherd leaves the ninety-nine to find the one that's gone astray and joyfully, lovingly carries her back to the fold. [31] The Father runs to embrace the smelly, shame-filled prodigal and welcomes him home.[32]

---

[29] Matthew 5:3
[30] Psalm 84:7
[31] Luke 15:3-7
[32] Luke 15:11-24

One evening I led our Imago Dei group in a meditation on this radical teaching of Jesus'. I wondered how to integrate what we'd just learned about our blessed condition with the sacrament of communion. A thought came.

"We often come to the Lord's table offering up our dark side to God. We are ashamed of it and want Christ to take it away along with our sins," I said. "Christ will indeed dispose of our sins, but he doesn't take away the parts of ourselves we don't like. God wants us to love our whole selves as much as God does."

That night we received the body of our Lord, broken for us. As we did we also received the One who loves and accepts our brokenness.

And God received us!

Jesus loved to eat with tax collectors and "sinners."[33] Here he was doing it again. Aren't we a bunch of lucky bums!

Your love, LORD, reaches to the heavens,
your faithfulness to the skies.
—Psalm36:5

---

[33] Matthew 9:11

THE COST OF LOVE

ALL THIS TALK about embracing our weaknesses is fine until someone gets hurt. I'm less inclined to romanticize the notion when I see how my failings have wounded others or how theirs have wounded me. When that happens, I'm tempted to hide behind a suit of armor.

Yet I can't love others without being vulnerable. And that isn't easy. I take a big risk when I allow people to see that I fear rejection, need approval, or desire control. Pharisees judge me; Moriartys exploit my weaknesses; and the offended pigeon-hole me ("Oh, there she goes, doing that annoying thing again"). Even if a person, as kindly as possible, tells me how my failings affect them, I still feel ashamed.

How do I embrace my weaknesses without feeling hurt?

I can't. It's the cost of love. It's the cost of taking up my cross and following Jesus.

A few weeks ago, while our Imago Dei group was in silent prayer, I remembered how our weaknesses endear us to Jesus. Then I sensed him inviting us to allow them to endear us to each other. That invitation shifted the focus from me to my neighbour.

Could I consider their shortcomings a precious part of them?

It wasn't long before a good friend went and did "that annoying thing" again and ruffled my feathers. My first instinct was to figure out how he could have done it differently. But I also discovered two deeper instincts: the desire to find the empathy to love him even more, and the urge to sit back and watch what

God would do. Often God does more in the process of smoothing feathers than if they'd never been ruffled in the first place.

If I'm going to talk about love on Valentine's Day, I want to move beyond romantic notions and talk about what real love is. Here is my amplified version of I Corinthians 13:4-7 *(Italics mine)*.

"Love is not self-seeking. It always protects *the vulnerable,* always trusts *that there is something bigger going on,* always hopes *that God will bring something good out of everything,* always perseveres *in the belief that this is the only way to live.*"

> *These three remain: faith, hope and love.*
> *But the greatest of these is love.*
> —1 Corinthians 13:13

JUDGMENT DAY

I COULDN'T BELIEVE my eyes. I got off the scale and on it again. The reading was the same.

It's been months since I've been to the gym. I knew I'd gained weight, but this was ten more pounds than I expected. Sheesh!

I stepped onto the cross-trainer and got to work. Thirty minutes went by at a snail's pace. I panted and tried not to stare at the slim, fit people around me. While I passed the time, I made a mental list of all the foods I would have to give up eating forever. Losing this weight was going to take a lot of time and persistence.

When the half hour was up, the machine congratulated me for burning 350 calories. Hmm. Only 34,650 more to go. And that's just the first ten pounds. I sat down for a while to catch my breath then wandered into the room with the free weights and another scale.

"Oh, what the heck," I thought holding a glimmer of hope that this scale would deliver better news.

I couldn't believe my eyes. I got off the scale and back on again. I weighed ten pounds less than I did on the previous scale. I wanted to kiss my new friend. Before I let myself get carried away, I went to the front desk and talked to the woman who'd checked me in. "I just weighed myself on both scales and . . ."

"Don't trust the first one you tried. It's really off. I keep telling the manager it needs to be recalibrated."

"Really?" My whole body lightened.

"Really."

"This one, in this room, is accurate?"

"That's right."

Wow. I lost ten pounds in thirty minutes. 35,000 calories gone. Poof!

I picked up a pair of five-pound dumbbells and pumped iron like I was Jillian Michaels—for a whole ten minutes. Because I could.

Out of Jesus' fullness, we have all received grace
in place of grace already given.
—John 1:16

Lent 2014

FACING THE PAGE

DEADLINES INTIMIDATE ME, especially when writing is involved. I've learned the wisdom of waiting for a wave of creativity to carry me and not struggle against the tide. But a deadline says, "Jump in and get going!"

Thursday afternoon I plunge into cold water that's over my head. Will my sermon come together by Sunday? This is my fear every time I write one, yet God always comes through. Isaiah 41:13 promises. "For I am the Lord your God who takes hold of your right hand and says to you, 'Do not fear; I will help you.'"

With a little more confidence, I begin to swim in the choppy sea of thoughts and words scratched out on bits of paper. An outline forms, then one paragraph after another.

On Friday, I face the page again. Which way is the current flowing today? I lift my hand to grasp God's and jump in. The word count hovers like a shiver of sharks. My sermon's way too long. I sigh and offer up one poetic bit, then another. I surface for lunch then dive back in. At three o'clock I get on my bike. Bruce Cockburn's "Pacing the Cage" plays in my head as I ride.

After supper, Fred relaxes with a book. Isn't this what Friday nights are for? I return to the page and attend to what emerged during my ride. Then I put the PowerPoint together. Images drift in. I exchange one find for another.

Saturday morning I have a two-hour window to practice out loud and time myself. The clock frowns. I feed the sharks again, take a deep breath and read it again. This time I catch a current of emotion when I hear myself talk about empathy. Word and image and sound and meaning converge; I feel solid ground under my feet.

Saturday night I turn the pages in my mind while I soak in the tub. Something's wrong with the last section, but I can't put my finger on it.

Three in the morning, I'm awake floating on the page again, and realize it's a structural problem. I dive down to fix it, reprint the page and go back to bed.

Sunday morning a few of us gather to pray before the service. After a moment of silence, one fellow says, as he often does, "I have a word from the Lord for you."

I'm listening.

"You are up high and must jump into the cold water below. You are afraid to jump, but a feather floats down from heaven and carries you with it."

His words remind me of a quote from Hildegard of Bingen that says, "I am a feather on the breath of God."

"God will be with you," he says.

And God was.

Listen: there was once a King sitting on his throne. Around him stood great and wonderfully beautiful columns ornamented with ivory, bearing the banners of the King with great honor. Then it pleased the King to raise a small feather from the ground and he commanded it to fly. The feather flew, not because of anything in itself but because the air bore it along. Thus am I a feather on the breath of God.
—Hildegard of Bingen, (1098-1179)

CLOSED FOR A REASON

WORDS BOUNCE OFF my heart like rain on pavement. Not just any words. God's words. They won't go in. I'm closed, locked up tight.

I sit with my Bible open on my lap and remember another time when I felt like this. We were on vacation in the arid little town of Osoyoos. I wrote,

After breakfast, we got into our friends' blue Honda and headed north. On the way, we passed a fruit stand with a red and white CLOSED sign on the door. The curtains were drawn, and I imagined the owner safely inside reading a paperback and sipping coffee. That's me: CLOSED. I've had enough truth for one season, thank you very much. I don't want to witness any more train wrecks or hear any more bad news from the TV, from the mirror, or my bathroom scales. I need no more evidence of how messed up we all are or how little I have to show for my life. I know "the truth shall set you free," but that's assuming you survive the shock of hearing it first. Solomon, in all his wisdom, should have added another verse to Ecclesiastes 3: "There is a season to be open and a season to be closed." I was certainly closed for the season.[34]

As I remember that time, I'm struck by two things. First is the fact that I noticed my desire to shut out both God and my

---

[34] Esther Hizsa, "Astronomical Units," *Stories of an Everyday Pilgrim*, 86.

feelings. Sometimes I can go along in life oblivious to the big CLOSED sign I'm wearing around my neck.

Second, there was a reason I was closed. Recent events triggered memories of others from long ago, and I didn't want to go there again. The steady drops of the truth they told turned into a downpour, and I quickly closed up shop.

I read the scripture passage again and search for a thought that might penetrate my heart.

This line does it: "Without you nothing makes sense."

I sit in the silence and open the door a crack, so God can slip in.

"What happened?" God's voice is soft and gentle. "Tell me, what's going on for you?"

God's questions, like the hand of Moses, strike the rock of my heart. Out gush my words, and God hears them all.

Keep me safe, O God,
I've run for dear life to you.
I say to GOD, "Be my Lord!"
Without you, nothing makes sense.
—Psalm 16:1, 2 (The Message)

THE DESIRE TO DISAPPEAR

"SOMETIMES I WISH I could disappear," I told Father Elton once while I was praying the Ignatian Spiritual Exercises last year.

"Of course you do," he said. "You want to do as you were told."

"What do you mean?" I asked.

"That memory you had of yourself as a toddler, when you were crying and your sibling squeezed your cheeks . . ."

The image returned in full force: I'm sitting on the couch with my mother beside me. She is holding our baby brother, and my four-year-old sister and six-year-old brother are in front of me. They're angry. One of them squeezes my cheeks together so hard I feel the flesh pressed against my teeth. I hear: "Be quiet! Nobody asked you to be here."

I inhaled deeply and returned to the present, to Father Elton's kind eyes and safe words.

"You were expected not to exist, something you couldn't do," he said.

"But I keep trying."

I remember the first time I was tempted by the delicious desire to disappear. I felt drawn to float away into an imaginary black hole where nothing was expected of me.

But under that temptation is a deeper desire: the desire to be heard, welcomed and comforted, the desire to be real and accepted.

God longs to fill these desires and prayer opens up a way for God to do it. That's why Ignatius asked retreatants praying the Retreat in Daily Life to spend an hour a day fully present to God.

Each morning, I would sit on the couch in my study and ask for the grace I needed to pray with a gospel story and imagine myself in it with Jesus. Then I talked with Jesus about what I saw or felt and listened to his response.

I met with Father Elton weekly and shared what I'd experienced in that dedicated time of prayer. "Jesus never seems to get tired of showing me how precious I am to him," I told Father Elton more than once.

Every time I did, he smiled and nodded, as if he could see me materializing before his very eyes.

Take delight in the Lord,
and he will give you the desires of your heart.
—Psalm 37:4

RESISTING THE SIRENS

I REMEMBER THE first time I identified the delicious desire to disappear. Sirens,[35] born of innocent angst, sang to me from the shore. They continue to this day, luring me out of life and into the snack cupboard and one television series after another.

Withdrawing from the world and enjoying a distraction or two can be a welcome break from stress, physical pain, or repetitive thoughts. But habitually retreating from reality takes its toll.

Excessive disappearances deaden my senses and dull my hearing. I become unmoved by beauty and unaware of tastes. I find myself not caring about people and stuff that matters. And I don't care that I don't care.

It's not depression. I made that diagnosis when I read Kathleen Norris's *Acedia & me*. It's acedia, a term used by the Desert Mothers and Fathers in the fourth century, which means "the absence of care."

Norris writes, "The desert monks termed acedia 'the noonday demon' because the temptation usually struck during the heat of the day, when the monk was hungry and fatigued, and susceptible to the suggestion that his commitment to a life of prayer was not worth the effort."[36]

---

[35] In Greek mythology, the Sirens were dangerous yet beautiful creatures, portrayed as femme fatales who lured nearby sailors with their enchanting music and voices to shipwreck on the rocky coast of their island.

[36] Kathleen Norris, *Acedia & me*, 5.

We too can suffer from the same affliction. Norris explains, "When life becomes too challenging and engagement with others too demanding, acedia offers a kind of spiritual morphine: you know the pain is there, yet can't rouse yourself to give a damn."[37]

Acedia preys upon us in weak moments and uses the lies and fears instilled in our childhood to undo us. The demon/Siren finally departs only after it has detached us from God and others.

If I don't want to drift onto the rocks of apathy, I need to reattach myself to God. I must turn my back to the beguiling Sirens and ground myself, as the trees do in Psalm 1. They are "planted by streams of water that yields fruit in due season, and their leaves flourish. And in all they do, they give life."[38]

So for Lent, I'm taking a break from my Netflix fiends and hanging out with Jesus and people who have unscripted lives.

"Shush!" I must say to the Sirens and choose, each day, to enter life instead of watching it.

Many are the heartaches of those
separated from Love;
Steadfast love abides with those
who surrender their lives
in the hands of the Beloved.
—Psalm 32:10[39]

---

[37] Kathleen Norris, *Acedia & me*, 3.
[38] Nan C. Merrill, *Psalms for Praying: An Invitation to Wholeness*, Psalm 1:3
[39] Ibid.

THE UNENDING MIRACLE OF LOVE

"MY HEART WAS strangely warmed," John Wesley wrote at Aldersgate in 1738 when he knew for certain that he was saved.

Two travellers on the road to Emmaus had a similar experience. While they didn't recognize the risen Christ walking with them, their hearts knew. They said later, "Were not our hearts burning within us while he talked with us on the road and opened the Scriptures to us?"[40]

I know what they're talking about because I've experienced this strange feeling in my heart. A sudden warm spaciousness fills my chest and elicits a tear or two whenever I sense that something is true and very important to God.

The important truth that sets my heart ablaze now is in these words from *The Cloud of Unknowing*.

It is God, and he alone, who can fully satisfy the hunger and longing of our spirit which transformed by God's redeeming grace is enabled to embrace him by love.[41]

I have often imagined God embracing me. But me, embrace God? The mystic continued,

No one can fully comprehend the uncreated God with his knowledge, but each one, in a different way, can grasp him fully through love.[42]

---

[40] Luke 24:32
[41] *The Cloud of Unknowing*, (edited by William Johnston), 50.
[42] Ibid.

I picture our six-year-old grandson, Hadrian. He was draped over Fred one Sunday in church with his soft cheek pressed against my husband's leathery one. One hand was cupped under his opa's chin and the other, fingers splayed, was buried in Fred's thick hair and massaging his scalp. A woman on the worship team looked up from her djembe drum and seeing such a display of affection was brought to tears.

Truly this is the unending miracle of love: that one loving person, through his love, can embrace God, whose being fills and transcends the entire creation.[43]

I close my eyes and open my heart to the image and words of the mystic. I imagine myself embracing God: my Father, my Mother. For a sacred, eternal moment, I rest my cheek on my Abba's leathery face and encircle God's neck with my arm. My spirit is satisfied as I caress God's temple and soak up Love's sighs with my fingers.

Afterward, whenever I returned to the thought of embracing God or the image of Hadrian and Fred, my heart is strangely warmed again. Truly this is an unending miracle.

We love because God first loved us.
—1 John 4:19.

---

[43] *The Cloud of Unknowing,* (edited by William Johnston), 50.

ARE YOU WITHERING ON THE VINE?

"ARE YOU SUFFERING from spiritual depletion?" Rob Des Cotes asked participants at the Soul Care retreat we hosted at our church. To help us answer that question, Rob led us through this diagnostic list.

Are you experiencing any of the following?

___ Loss of peace (unable to relax or rest from busy thoughts)

___ Loss of receptiveness (unable to receive/enjoy people, nature, art, etc.)

___ Loss of self-control (no "off" switch, unable to step back and make healthy choices)

___ Less capacity for relating well with others and God (feel like the "tail wags the dog," no distance between you and your fear)

___ Less capacity for restoration (like rechargeable batteries that have lost their capacity to recharge)

I checked off five out of five. My life was packed to the edges. I rushed through morning quiet times or skipped them. I ate lunch while I worked. In the evening, when I did have time to pray, I was exhausted, and acedia persuaded me to have a snack and watch my favorite TV show instead. I still had moments of connecting with God, but that wasn't enough to fend off the growing dissipation.

"If you are answering 'yes' to most of these statements, you may be withering on the vine," Rob told us. "Jesus said, 'I am the vine; you are the branches. If you remain in me and I in you, you will bear much fruit; but apart from me you can do nothing."[44]

When we get too busy to spend time with God, we are like a severed branch. No longer attached to the vine, it cannot obtain the water and nutrients it needs to survive. This old hymn captures the truth,

> *I need Thee, oh, I need Thee;*
> *Every hour I need Thee;*
> *Oh, bless me now, my Saviour,*
> *I come to Thee.*[45]

I am thankful for Lent, this season of repentance and renewal. I am thankful for Rob and the gentle way he calls us back to rest in God. And I am thankful for Jesus who revives me and invites me to abide in him again.

> *As the Father has loved me, so I have loved you;*
> *abide in my love.*
> —John 15:9 (NRSV)

---

[44] John 15:5

[45] Annie S. Hawkes and Robert Lowry, "I Need Thee Every Hour," 1872.

Palm Sunday 2014

MOVING FROM "ME" TO "WE"

IF I WERE Jesus riding into Jerusalem, I would have been pretty agitated.[46] Imagine entering the city where you're about to be betrayed, abandoned, beaten, and killed. How could Jesus remain present to the crowds of joyous people shouting, "Hosanna!"? Before the week is through, another crowd will shout, "Crucify him." Yet Jesus remains calm as he rides into Jerusalem and is welcomed by hundreds of palm-waving supporters. He seemed to savour the moment.

How does he do that? How does anyone welcome the reality of the moment without having the reality of life rob them of joy? I got an answer to my question at Rob Des Cotes' Soul Care retreat.

Rob said, "This is how we tend to go through life." Then he drew a straight horizontal line on a flip chart. He wrote "God" on the left end and "Me" on the right. Then above it, he drew a question mark. He then joined the ends of the solid line with dotted lines to the question mark to make a triangle (what I call the "me" stance).

He pointed to the question mark. "We have a relationship with something—an event, a person, a job, a goal, or a problem—and then we ask God to help us or bless what we're doing. God is distant from us," he said.

Then Rob drew a second triangle. But this time the solid line was vertical, with "God" written at the top of the line and "Me"

---

[46] Mark11:1-11

at the bottom. He drew a question mark to the right of the line and connected the three points as before with two dotted lines (the "we" stance).

Rob pointed to the second diagram. "Instead, Jesus welcomes us to re-establish our relationship with God daily then, together with God, relate to everything else in our lives."

Jesus was able to ride into Jerusalem and lovingly interact with the people around him because his primary relationship was not with his inevitable suffering and death. It was with God. The Lord God was holding Jesus' right hand and telling him, "Do not fear, I myself am with you. We will face what is ahead together."

When I think of addressing life this way—from a "we" stance instead of a "me" stance—I feel hopeful and light. I relax. I don't have to be prepared for every possible outcome when the God of the universe is beside me. I can step back from whatever I'm dealing with and be more present to those around me.

It's comforting to know I can turn to Jesus at any moment and say, "I'm glad you're here."

For I am the Lord your God
who takes hold of your right hand
and says to you, Do not fear;
I will help you…
I myself will help you," declares the Lord,
your Redeemer, the Holy One of Israel.
—Isaiah 41:13, 14

Maundy Thursday 2014

STAY WITH ME

AN ANGEL COMFORTED Jesus in his anguish.[47] He longed for such compassion from his friends, but they couldn't do it. They disappeared into a panacea of sleep. We rely on Jesus to be with us in everything, but will we be with him in all he must endure?

Last year on Maundy Thursday, I was praying the Ignatian Exercises, when Jesus said, "Esther, stay with me."

I swallowed hard and asked God for the grace to do it. Then I closed my eyes and imagined myself in the Garden of Gethsemane.

Jesus is about to be betrayed; his heart is heavy with sorrow. Peter, James and John are asleep, deaf to his painful pleading. I want to put my hands over my ears. It's heart-wrenching to hear Jesus so deeply distressed. He paces and cries out, "Please . . . Father . . . take this cup from me." He falls on his knees, covers his face with his hands, and wails.

"God, do something!" No sooner do I say the words when an angel appears at his side.

I ask God, "Can I go and comfort him too?"

"Go," God says.

I run to Jesus and wrap my arms around him. He clutches on to me so tightly I can barely breathe. He trembles. His tears soak into my shirt.

After a while, he sits back and looks me in the eyes. "My Father has asked me to go to the cross and die for you," he says wiping his cheeks. "And I will go."

---

[47] Luke 22:43

"Don't do it for me," I say, "Am I really worth it?"

"Are you worth it?" He shakes his head. "How could you be with me all this time and still not know that you are the treasure of great price, the pearl that I have sold everything for? The thought of not being with you forever is what convinced me to say yes. I will do it for you, and for them (he looks at the sleeping disciples), for everyone."

I touch his face and kiss his wet cheek. I hold his hands and rub the spot where the nails will enter. "Remember my touch when you are dying," I say. "May that memory soften the pain."

"Thank you," Jesus says and hugs me. "I'm glad you're here."

Then he says to us, "My soul is overwhelmed with sorrow to the point of death. Stay here and keep watch with me."[48]

Stay with me; remain here with me.
Watch and pray,
watch and pray.
—Jacques Brethier[49]

---

[48] Matthew 26:38
[49] Jacques Brethier, "Stay with Me," Taizé Community.

WITH CHRIST IN GLORY

I LOOK AT the naked, bloodied body next to me. "What's he doing here?"

A sinless man is being crucified beside us: me on his left, the other criminal on his right. The crucified always die in disgrace, our lives held up as negative examples.

Yet, he is good. People called him rabbi, healer, messiah, saviour, Son of God. At birth, they called him Emmanuel: "God with us." God with us in life. Now, God with us in death.

Crowds hurl insults at Jesus, insults we deserve. The other thief joins in. "Some saviour he is. Can't even save himself, let alone us."

"Have some respect." I struggle for breath. "We had it coming, but not him. He's not like us."

"He's a fake."

"No. A king." Lungs burn, limbs scream. Always knew I'd get caught, die alone. But I'm not alone. I'm with the one they call . . .

"Jesus." I can barely whisper. "Remember me when you come into your kingdom."

Jesus turns his head and looks at me. I see his face for the first time. He's no older than I am. Blood trickles down from the crown of thorns on his head. His voice is gentle. "Today," he says between breaths, "you will be with me in paradise."[50]

---

[50] Luke 23:43

Euphoria rises from my belly, shoots into every sinew and cell in my body, erupts in laughter. Never before have I felt such love, such joy.

Then suddenly, it's dark. Mid-afternoon, can't see a thing. The earth heaves and groans. Nails rip flesh. Cries, curses, prayers. Hold breath. Silence.

Is he gone?

Jesus cries, "Father, into your hands I commit my spirit." One breath and—wait. No more.

I am alone again. But not alone.

Tears on my cheeks. Paradise. Today. I'm coming home to the King.

Do you think anyone is going to be able
to drive a wedge between us and Christ's love for us?
There is no way!
Not trouble, not hard times,
not hatred, not hunger,
not homelessness, not bullying threats,
not backstabbing,
not even the worst sins listed in Scripture.
—Romans 8:34, 35 (The Message)

Holy Saturday 2014

HOMELESS

they take
him
down from the cross
his
     cold body pierced
     bruised mouth silenced
     soft eyes blind

as he began
now at end
     wrapped in cloth strips
     laid in wrong place
helpless
God

stone heaved
tomb sealed
sudden scream
     mine

guards curse
push me
     "Go home!"

can't

have none
     but
     him

Easter 2014

THE INCREDULITY OF THOMAS

Words are wasted on his
impenetrable mind:
"Unless I see,
unless I touch."[51]

Incredulity
guards the heart
seals the tomb
from disappointment.

"Thomas!"
Voice charged,
words spark.
"See.
Touch."

Incredulity
reaches out,
flesh toward flesh
until—

hope arcs
current flows.

One mind, one heart, one joy.

---

[51] John 20:24-29
Title of poem is from "The Incredulity of St. Thomas" by Caravaggio, 1601-2.

GO PRAY OUTSIDE

EVERYWHERE NEW LIFE is emerging from winter's tomb: cherry trees blossom, goslings waddle in a row, baby birds chirp from their nests. The earth is not silent; it joyously proclaims, "Christ has risen. He has risen indeed."

The first mandate God gave us was to tend Earth's glorious garden and the many creatures that live in it. Thousands of years later, Jesus commanded us to love God and love our neighbour. That doesn't mean we forget our original calling to care for creation. Jesus said that those two commands sum up all the others, including the very first one. [52] What we love, we will care for.

Go pray outside. Celebrate Earth Day with your neighbours: the succulent shrub and blossoming vine, as well as ants, beavers, and eagles. Join the choir of birds, light and lilies that declare their Maker's praise, breathe life on the earth, and still our hearts with awe.

This is my Father's world,
the birds their carols raise,
the morning light, the lily white,
declare their maker's praise.
— Maltbie D. Babcock[53]

---

[52] John 12:24; Genesis 2:15; Luke 10:27
[53] Maltbie D. Babcock, "This Is My Father's World," 1901.

A RETREAT WITH GOD

"LEAVE YOUR LAPTOP at home," God said as I packed for a three-day retreat on Bowen Island. "Just come and be with me."

"But I can't write much without my electronic friend," I responded.

I think that was the point.

My job was to rest and pray. Not very exciting. Every day I kept waiting for something to happen, but I didn't have any breakthroughs or prophetic insights. My soul asked me what I was feeling. The anticlimactic answer was: relaxed. Acting as my own spiritual director, I pressed in. "Do you have a sense of how God is feeling about that?" I asked myself.

"Pleased, I suppose."

I sat on a rock by the shore and watched the birds. They were more restless than I was. One or another was always fluttering their wings or changing allegiances. A seal popped her head up and then disappeared. The clouds shifted, ferries came and went, as I watched and waited with God.

Back at the cottage where I was staying, I sipped Rooibos tea and opened the book, *No Crowds Present*. I felt my heart strangely warmed when I read this:

> *Author and speaker Brennan Manning tells the story of an Irish priest who, on a walking tour of a rural parish, sees an old peasant kneeling by the side of the road praying.*

Impressed, the priest says to the man, "You must be very close to God.

The peasant looks up from his prayers, thinks for a moment, and then smiles and replies, "Yes, he is very fond of me." [54]

Jesus looked at him and loved him.
—Mark 10:21

---

[54] Mike Stewart, *No Crowds Present*, 35.

THIN PLACES

SOME PLACES ARE sacred to me: Bowen Island, Battleship Islands on Garibaldi Lake, and Black Sage Road that weaves through the vineyards between Oliver and Osoyoos. Each place evokes a visceral memory of an encounter with God. These experiences were so profound that my body remembers them with a flutter of awe whenever I imagine myself there.

"A favorite place of mine is a particular trail and beach on Vancouver Island near Tofino," writes Mike Stewart, an Anglican priest. "Every time I visit the area, I am touched again by God's friendship. Once when I was staying with friends there, I had a sudden desire to visit the trail and beach. In my heart, I knew Jesus was waiting for me to get there. As I walked the beach alone, I heard him speaking to me in the ocean wind, 'I will always be your friend.' 'Lord,' I replied, 'And I yours.'"[55]

"I know a place
where God dwells," the heart whispers.
"Let's go there."

"Why, God is
everywhere," the head replies.
"There's no place where God is not."

"Yes," says the heart, "but there are thin places
where earth and heaven touch.
God is waiting for us there.'[56]

---

[55] Mike Stewart, *No Crowds Present, 40.*
[56] Poem "Thin Places" by Esther Hizsa

GOD IS IN LOVE WITH YOU

"ASK CHRISTIANS WHAT they believe about God," David Benner writes in *Surrender to Love*, "and most have a good deal to say. However, ask the same people what they know about God from direct personal experience, and most will have much less to say."[57]

Perhaps you're one with little to say. If that's the case, take a few minutes to ask the Holy Spirit to show you how God has loved you today.

You don't need to think hard. Just wait. The Holy Spirit will bring something to mind. It could be the way a co-worker made you smile or how a sunflower looked ready to burst. Perhaps it was finding that pair of sunglasses you thought you'd lost. Whatever comes to mind, savour that moment. Thank God for it.

Benner says, "God is head-over-heels in love with you. God is simply giddy about you. God just can't help loving you. And God loves you deeply, recklessly and extravagantly—just the way you are."[58]

God is ready to burst with deep, reckless affection for you. So pay attention.

Before you know it, you'll be quoting the poet Hafiz.

---

[57] David G. Benner, *Surrender to Love*, 27.
[58] Ibid, 18.

TWO GIANT FAT PEOPLE

God and I have become
Like two giant fat people
Living in a tiny boat.
We keep
Bumping into each other
And laughing.
—Hafiz[59]

---

[59] Hafiz, *Love Poems from God, Twelve Voices from the East and West* (translated by Daniel Ladinsky).

GOD'S EXUBERANT, UNCONTAINABLE LOVE

GOD'S CRAZY ABOUT us. I'm riveted to this theme. God's exuberance is uncontainable.

Recently I stumbled upon this quote by Henri Nouwen, "God does not require a pure heart before embracing us. Even if we return only because following our desires has failed to bring happiness, God will take us back . . . 'Come,' God says, 'let me wipe your tears, and let my mouth come close to your ear and say to you, "I love you. I love you. I love you."'"[60]

God went on to illustrate these words. My family was already seated at church one Sunday when I came into the sanctuary. As soon as my granddaughter, Hannah, saw me, she lit up. She patted the empty chair beside her. When I sat there, she put her arms around me and snuggled up. A friend seated behind us saw Hannah's loving gesture and said to me, "That was God, you know, welcoming you." There were tears in her eyes when she said it.

The next day another friend told me how long ago God spoke to her through a verse in Isaiah. "My delight is in you," she'd heard God say to her heart. For years she marvelled at the fact that God lights up whenever God sees her.

"But today, when I remembered those words, I heard something different," she went on to say. "This time I heard, 'My delight is inside you—hidden there like a treasure.'"

---

[60] Henri Nouwen, *Show Me the Way: Daily Lenten Readings*

Soon afterward, I heard a priest talk about how to discern God's voice. Father Richard Soo said, "If you hear the thought *I love you*, it's God. If you hear *I forgive you*, it's God. And if you hear *I love you again*, it's God telling you again, because God likes to tell us often, and God knows we didn't believe it the first time."

Everywhere we go birds are singing and flowers are whispering a message from our creator: *I love you. I love you. I love you.*

You shall no more be termed Forsaken,
and your land shall no more be termed Desolate;
but you shall be called My Delight is in Her . . .
for the Lord delights in you . . .
—Isaiah 62:4 (NRSV)

RESURRECTION CLEANERS

JESUS HAS BEEN spring-cleaning my heart, soul and mind. Resurrection energy has him showing up everywhere. At all hours of the day and night, I see his van parked outside. Within minutes he and his heavenly team are pulling back curtains, opening up windows, and refreshing my house with love.

He showed up at Imago Dei as we reflected on a poem by Margaret Avison. He used her words to implore us to "fall anew in ever-new depths of skywashed Love."

As we entered into a time of silent prayer, I wanted to receive God's "skywashed Love," but a tempest of remorse distracted me. I couldn't get my mind off my friend "Mary." I had unintentionally done something that upset her. I caused that, I kept thinking.

"No, you didn't," Jesus interjected. "I let it happen."

He paused and then added, "I'm renovating your souls to make more room for my love. Don't worry. She'll be fine."

Just like that, the grey clouds of shame were swept aside, and I was enveloped in endless blue peace.

Spring is here and Jesus is cleaning out cupboards and drawers and lining them with loving kindness. That means those old blaming thoughts and false beliefs must go. He bags them up, clanking and banging, and takes them to the curb.

This morning as I was praying, I heard him call out, "I found another one!" He held it up then flung it in the trash.

"I love you. I love you. I love you," he sang.

you implore
me to so fall
in Love, and fall anew in
ever-new depths of skywashed Love till every
capillary of your universe
throbs with rivering fire
—Margaret Avison[61]

---

[61] Margaret Avison, "The Word," *The Country of the Risen King: An Anthology of Christian Poetry.*

Ascension Day 2014

CHRIST WILL COME AGAIN

THE DISCIPLES WERE anxious, afraid and extremely sad as they watched Jesus whisked up to heaven. What would they do now?

He promised he wouldn't leave them alone, that God would send the Holy Spirit. But how could this Spirit possibly replace Jesus? What could take the place of seeing his face, hearing his voice, or feeling his arm around their shoulders? How were they supposed to follow Jesus now?

We can relate to their anguish. We go along in the Christian life experiencing God in a certain way. We find a rhythm that works. We know how to pray, how to live, where to go, and what to do. Then suddenly one day it stops working. Jesus seems to have left the building. Often it's at a time when we need him most.

We pray harder, spend more time in scripture, and repent of everything we can think of. We may even read books or take a class, but nothing seems to rekindle the spiritual life we once had.

Disorienting darkness descends. When it persists, we may be tempted to give up on church, God and the whole darn thing.

After Christ ascended, the disciples kept looking up at the empty sky. Finally, the angels shooed them away. Jesus would come again in glory at the end of time, but meanwhile, God had something new in store for them.

God has something new in store for us as well.

Early on in his ministry, Jesus told a mystified Pharisee, "You should not be surprised at my saying, 'You must be born again.'"[62]

When we find ourselves in the dark, perhaps we're in a birth canal. Maybe God is about to deliver us into a whole new way of being. Once the disciples stopped looking back to what they had and looked forward to Christ's coming anew, some pretty exciting stuff happened.

Do not leave Jerusalem,
but wait for the gift my Father promised,
which you have heard me speak about.
For John baptized with water,
but in a few days you will be baptized with the Holy Spirit.
—Acts 1:4, 5

---

[62] John 3:7

REBORN

I'VE BEEN BORN again and again. With each new spiritual birth, I emerge from darkness into light as helpless as a babe. How does this new life in Christ work?

In the past month, I've been reborn into the reality of God's delight in all of us. I had gotten so used to clambering about loaded down with other people's disappointments and expectations—not to mention my own—that I experienced more desolation than joy. Now God is inviting me to shed the heavy layers of gloom and live lightly.

But how do I do that when things keep going wrong?

I was thinking about this during a long bike ride. I had to go over the Alex Fraser Bridge to get to Tsawwassen, but couldn't find the cyclists' access. The signs were confusing and the map didn't help. What I need, I half-prayed, is someone to guide me.

I hadn't seen any cyclists for a while, but at that moment, lo and behold, one showed up. And it was Scott, someone I knew from my days at Regent College. What were the odds of that?

"Follow me." He showed me the path and went on his way.

I asked myself as I rode around Burns Bog and along Boundary Bay, why did that happen? Was God promising to do the same thing in my spiritual life? It seemed too easy. But really, there's more chance of God showing up when needed than Scott.

I have been reborn from above yet God is right here. Like a devoted mother, a protective father, God is guiding me every step of the way.

Jesus replied, "Very truly I tell you,
no one can see the kingdom of God
unless they are born again."
—John 3:3

Pentecost 2014

A MIRACLE DAY

THEY WERE FILLED with the Holy Spirit. Not just some believers, but all of them.

> *When the day of Pentecost came, they were all together in one place. Suddenly a sound like the blowing of a violent wind came from heaven and filled the whole house where they were sitting. They saw what seemed to be tongues of fire that separated and came to rest on each of them. All of them were filled with the Holy Spirit and began to speak in other tongues as the Spirit enabled them.*[63]

It was the miracle of the loaves and the fishes all over again. Jesus was raised up to heaven and multiplied. Now there was plenty of him to go around and they were filled to overflowing.[64]

Before that day, the Holy Spirit came to special people at special times: David when he was chosen to be king of Israel, Mary at the conception of Jesus, Zechariah when he prophesied at the naming of his son, John.[65]

But from then on all believers were given Jesus' Spirit.

This means we never have to do anything on our own ever again. This means, as *The Message* says in Romans 8:12-14,

---

[63] Acts 2:1-4
[64] John 6: 1-15
[65] 1 Samuel 16:13; Luke 1:35, 67

We don't owe this old do-it-yourself life one red cent. There's nothing in it for us, nothing at all. The best thing to do is give it a decent burial and get on with your new life. God's Spirit beckons. There are things to do and places to go!

Whatever is going on for us, whatever we face, big or small, Jesus' Spirit is there. Within us, he listens with compassion and feels what we feel, amplifying our joy and embracing our sorrow. Patiently, gently, the Spirit brings thoughts or memories to mind, that open our eyes to see what God sees and leads us forward. Then—oh my heart—our Companion goes with us! Together we do things and go places we never thought possible.

Christ. In us. It's a miracle day.

I will ask the Father, and he will give you another advocate
to help you and be with you forever
—the Spirit of truth.
—John 14:16, 17

SWEET FREEDOM

I PREACHED AFTER a particularly full week and three restless nights. I was tired but felt confident. I had practised my sermon out loud without relying much on my notes and looked forward to doing it like that on Sunday. However, when I got behind the pulpit and in front of everyone, self-doubt surfaced and glued me to my notes.

I know this intro. What am I doing? I thought.

I looked up and wanted to step back, but I was tethered in place by the microphone. One end was pinned to my collar and the other rested on the pulpit since I didn't have a way of clipping it onto me. I felt leashed to a nervous insecurity that questioned me about incidental facts. A few times I stumbled over my words and was sidetracked by thoughts.

After church, preoccupation with my performance had me wound up tight. "Did it go all right?" I asked Fred more than once. "Yes," he said looking me in the eyes.

During a walk that afternoon, I unwound the event with trepidation. I enjoyed what worked well and most of the sermon did. But it was hard to accept what didn't and the fact that there was nothing I could do about it now.

"I long for the freedom to just preach without insecurity hampering me," I told Fred. "I tried my hardest."

That thought triggered a memory from elementary school. The teacher took our class to the gym and lined us up along its perimeter. He asked us to run across it diagonally, one at a time. I was not an athlete and my peers and teacher would be watching. I ran as fast as I could, unaware of how loudly my feet pounded on the floor. As I caught my breath, the teacher remarked, "Sounds like you were stomping grapes." Everyone laughed. I felt like a fool.

But no one was laughing now. Why did that memory return?

Before I went to bed that night, I sat down to pray. I allowed myself to be present to the Holy Spirit who was present to me. My Companion was gentle and compassionate, matching sigh with sigh.

The next morning, when I returned to pray, I saw things differently. The freedom the Holy Spirit longed to give me, was not the freedom to live unhampered by self-doubt but the freedom not to care if I stomped or not.

Yes, that's the sweet freedom I want.

Guard us, Lord, from seeking to find our identity
in performance or professions.
—Rob Peterson,
SoulStream Community's Noon Prayer[66]

---

[66] See Appendix 1 for SoulStream's Daily Prayers

ARE YOU GOING TO WEAR IT?

IT WASN'T MY outfit that offended; it was my belief.

After the disgruntled person walked away, a friend remains and asks me if I'm okay.

"I think I've just been shamed," I say.

"Are you going to wear it?" he asks.

His question startles and relieves me. I have a choice. I don't have to accept the heavy judgment placed on me.

I had talked about this with Karen in spiritual direction a few weeks before.

"I seem to collect other people's fears and judgments," I'd said. "I get so weighed down by it all." Then I told her about a particular incident that had upset me.

As we sat in God's presence, I saw myself draped in a heavy coat of fear. Jesus, filled with compassion, lifted the ill-fitting coat off my shoulders. As he did, I realized that the coat didn't fit because it wasn't mine.

"Are you going to wear it?" Jesus asked me then and again now. I don't have to feel ashamed for having a different opinion than someone else. I can let it go.

As I do, peace returns and joy too. I feel grateful for my friend and for God, who allowed the timely exchange.

Even though I have been reborn into God's delight, coats of shame, fear and judgment—of all shapes and colors—are still thrust on me. I refuse one and the next day four more descend. Goodness, has there been a sale on ugly coats?

I breathe in and out slowly.
No matter. I'd rather leave a trail of coats than wear them.

It is for freedom that Christ has set us free.
Stand firm, then,
and do not let yourselves be burdened again
by a yoke of slavery.
—Galatians 5:1

HOW WILL YOU WEAR THAT?

IT ISN'T JUST fear, shame and judgment that are placed on me. I receive compliments too. People often thank me for something I've done or tell me how a certain blog post has impacted them. But it's hard for me to take it in without imagining what they didn't say. Does that mean they didn't like the previous posts?

On other occasions, approval can go to my head, and all I think about is how I can get more.

I talked about that too in spiritual direction.

"I had my first day as the new intern facilitator of Living from the Heart," I said.

Karen smiled. "How was it?"

"Wonderful. Jeff and Deb told me, more than once, how much they enjoy working with me. Ten years ago, Jeff's book was the first one I read when I began my degree at Regent College and now we're colleagues."

She waited for me to say more.

"I like these affirmations and hold onto them tightly. I'm afraid someone is going to come along and say something that will knock my feet out from under me," I said, feeling tears come.

"And when you imagine Jesus with you?" she asked.

I closed my eyes for a moment and got a sense of what Jesus felt. "He's thrilled that people see what he sees."

"So what will you do with their praise?"

Again I closed my eyes and asked Jesus that question. All of a sudden I knew. "It's dessert," I said. "I can't make a steady diet of it, but I can enjoy every bite."

"It's sweet," Karen added.

As I biked home from my spiritual direction session, I wondered how I would wear people's accolades. I don't want to reject them like the heavy coats of judgment and shame. But how do I wear a chocolate ganache tartlet or crème caramel? Perhaps, compliments are more like hats or scarves. They're not essential, but they highlight who we are.

Consider how the wildflowers grow.
They do not labor or spin.
Yet I tell you, not even Solomon in all his splendour
was dressed like one of these.
—Luke 12:27

SOMETHING EXCITING IS HAPPENING ON YOUR BLOCK

CHESTER FILBERT IS not happy. The title of the children's book written by Ellen Raskin about him explains why: *Nothing Ever Happens on My Block.*

The reader soon discovers, however, that the joke's on him because a lot happens on Chester's street. While he sits there moping, firemen put out a fire, police catch a thief, a gardener finds a treasure and so on.

Just like Chester, we often feel like nothing ever happens in our lives that draws us close to God. Other people have amazing experiences of God, but—sigh—not us.

That uncontainable love of God is spilling out all over the place, yet we hardly notice it. To help us become aware of God's love, we can use Ignatius of Loyola's Prayer of Examen (or Daily Examen). For five centuries people have found this simple prayer practice invaluable. We can do it while commuting, going for a walk or before falling asleep at night.

Here's how it's done. Take five minutes and ask the Holy Spirit to bring to mind a moment in the past day or week for which you were most grateful. Perhaps you forgot where you parked your car and found it anyway or maybe you were touched by what someone did or said to you. Whatever it was, take time to enjoy that moment again with Jesus.

In "God's Exuberant, Uncontainable Love," I mentioned a time when I was in church and God welcomed me home with a hug from my granddaughter. When it happened, I couldn't take it in; there was too much going on. But the next day in my prayer of Examen, I returned to that moment with Jesus and, as Mary did at Jesus' birth, treasured what happened in my heart.

As we practice the Daily Examen, we soon discover that Jesus has indeed "moved into the neighbourhood." He's on Chester's block, and yours and mine too. How exciting is that?

The Word became flesh and blood,
and moved into the neighborhood.
We saw the glory with our own eyes,
the one-of-a-kind glory,
like Father, like Son,
Generous inside and out,
true from start to finish.
—John 1:14 (The Message)

BURIED TREASURE

IT'S ALL FINE to recall those moments for which we are most grateful and treasure them in our hearts. But what about the events in our day for which we are least grateful? Who wants to treasure those? I'd just as soon forget them.

But Ignatius of Loyola believed uncomfortable moments contain treasures too. Experiences of desolation are included in our Daily Examen because God is there.

Psalm 23:4 says, "Yea, though I walk through the valley of the shadow of death, I will fear no evil; for you are with me; your rod and your staff, they comfort me."

It's easy to imagine God with us when life is free and easy. But the psalmist tells us that when we go through hard times, God has not abandoned us.

Father Richard Soo, a Jesuit priest, says that we often feel like we go through dark valleys alone. However, as we return to those places with Jesus in the Prayer of Examen, we will see how God was with us. What's more, when we linger there with Jesus, we can receive the comfort and protection God promised.

In "Sweet Freedom," I described how I went through a dark valley after preaching one Sunday. The next morning, as I returned to that desolation with Jesus, I saw things a different way. I appreciated the new insight, but what I treasured most was the compassionate way Jesus was with me in the darkness.

There's a consolation buried under every desolation. We discover it as we pray the second part of the Daily Examen.

Here's how it's done. After you've enjoyed revisiting a grateful moment with Jesus, take another five minutes and ask the Holy Spirit to bring to mind the moment in your day for which you were least grateful. Picture yourself with Jesus and relive that experience with the One who is kind and gentle of heart. What do you notice as you are with him? What is Jesus feeling?

If you imagine yourself being cornered by a finger-pointing frustrated guy in a beard and a robe, that's not Jesus. It's someone in your past pretending to be him.

Jesus—the real Jesus—looks at us and loves us. He knows we are standing on buried treasure, and he will help us find it.

But Mary treasured up all these things
and pondered them in her heart.
—Luke 2:19

ME AND MY SHADOW

I'M HESITANT TO confess this to you because when I do, you will find evidence that it's true. And where that leads, well, that makes me both nervous and hopeful. So here it is: I'm pretty self-centered.

I often put myself first and orchestrate my life to get what I want. Even if I do things for others, it's still about me and my shadow and the sweet little dance routine we have going.

When I see this ungodly trait in me, I want to get rid of it. But my shadow refuses to leave, stuck to me "like wallpaper sticks to the wall, like the seashore clings to the sea."[67]

Help me, Lord! I pray. But instead of getting rid of my shadow, God embraces it. In *Surrender to Love*, David Benner says, it isn't just the good side of us that God wants to love, but our dark side too. The Holy Spirit invites us to be vulnerable and snuggle with God in our untransformed state.

Benner writes, "For love to transform us, not only must we meet in vulnerability, we must also linger long enough for it to penetrate our woundedness. Snuggling keeps us in contact with love long enough that it has that effect."[68]

One evening, after my Examen offered more proof of my selfish ways, I read another chapter of Benner's book. In it, he too confessed that he struggles with self-centeredness. I sat there in awe: I was not alone.

---

[67] Billy Rose, "Me and My Shadow" (1927).
[68] David G. Benner, *Surrender to Love*, 53.

That night I lay in bed with the confidence I needed to expose my shadow side to God. The cavity it had created in me seemed as big as the Grand Canyon. I felt the Holy Spirit tremble with delight. "Thank you," God whispered, "for giving me such a huge space to fill with my love."

Then Love, bigger than the Grand Canyon filled and enveloped me and my shadow. We snuggled up into it and I fell asleep in God's arms.

Thank You that You lovingly accept us as we are
and invite us to rest in the intimacy of that love.
—Rob Peterson,
SoulStream Community's Noon Prayer [69]

---

[69] See Appendix 1 for SoulStream's Daily Prayers

WASTING MONEY

EVERY TIME I turned around, something was costing more money—a haircut, local produce, a restaurant meal. The matinée performance of a show Fred and I wanted to go to was sold out. Should we pay more for an evening performance?

We don't have a lot of money, so we're careful with it. Fred and I talked about the tickets and our recent expenditures as we walked to Imago Dei. "I think I see a pattern emerging," I said. "I wonder if God is answering my prayer to help me become less self-centered. Instead of whining about the cost, I could enjoy the fact that others are getting what they need."

"Besides," I continued, "in the Ignatian prayer I've been praying, I give all that I have back to God anyway."

That evening, the person leading invited us to use our imagination to pray with the story of the woman who anointed Jesus with perfume.[70] "What is Jesus asking you to 'waste' for him?" she asked.

I imagined myself as the woman with the alabaster jar of perfume. I resonated with the disciples' dismay: What a waste! Should I do it? Nervously I poured the expensive perfume on Jesus' head. The scent filled the room and delighted him. It delighted me, too.

Then the scene changed. I saw myself with Jesus pouring perfumed blessings on the people at Pacific Theatre, and then on

---

[70] Matthew 26:6-14

my hairstylist, the strawberry farmers, and the friend I had lunch with. Each person was filled with joy.

As Fred and I walked home, we talked about the evening and the sold-out matinée. "I want to spend more money and get the evening tickets," I said. He agreed.

Take, Lord, and receive all my liberty,
my memory, my understanding,
and my entire will,
All I have and call my own.
You have given all to me.
To you, Lord, I return it.
Everything is yours; do with it what you will.
Give me only your love and your grace,
that is enough for me.
—Ignatius of Loyola

THE REAL STORY BEGINS

I WAS AS restless as a cat. I'd pack a few things then check my emails. I looked over the list of items to bring to the SoulStream Partners' Annual Retreat. Check. Check. What? A photograph of myself? Why hadn't I noticed that before? Found one the wrong size; it would have to do. Pushed my nervousness aside. Checked my blog. Put my bag by the door. Ready, not ready.

The traffic was stop and go. I breathed in and out and arrived in plenty of time. Smiling faces welcomed me.

When everyone had gathered in the meeting room, we took turns introducing ourselves. After each introduction, we pinned the photo we brought to a board entitled SoulStream. Faces on the board and around the room reassured me: I belong here.

Over wine and cheese, I caught up with people I met last year and met new friends. I enjoyed the evening but woke in the night feeling anxious. I was afraid of something but didn't know what. "Welcome it," I sensed God say. "Listen to what it wants to tell you."

With that, my fear curled up and went to sleep.

The next day I made a collage while my fear purred quietly on my lap. I was drawn to images and words that reconnected me to who I was before I went to elementary school, before I learned to recreate myself to match the approval of others.

A picture of a little girl wearing swimming goggles caught my attention. She had an apple on her head and stuck out her tongue. I could almost hear her giggles and sing-song, "Na, na, na, na, na."

I cut out the phrases IF YOU ONLY KNEW WHAT WAS IN and THE REAL STORY and glued them onto the page along with the word BEGINS and a picture of a blue, blue ocean.

I felt as peaceful as that ocean for the remainder of the weekend. But the nameless fear returned when I got home. It meowed in the night.

The next day I was meditating on Peter's miraculous release from prison in Acts 12. I imagined myself as Peter. The angel whispered, "Let's get out of here." The chains fell off and I stepped over the sleeping guards and out of the fear that imprisoned me. I knew it now: the fear of rejection.

I'm beginning a new adventure. God is leading me into deeper, bluer freedom that I haven't known since I was a child. "Can you imagine the freedom of remaining who you are no matter what another face tells you?" God asks me. "That's where we're going."

God told them, "I've never quit loving you and never will.
Expect love, love, and more love!
And so now I'll start over with you and build you up again,
dear virgin Israel.
You'll resume your singing,
grabbing tambourines and joining the dance.
—Jeremiah 31:3, 4 (The Message)

ONE UNCOMFORTABLE ADVENTURE

I'M ON AN adventure into the deeper, bluer freedom of being myself.

Yeah. Right.

In Tolkien's *The Hobbit*, Gandalf said to Bilbo. "I am looking for someone to share in an adventure that I am arranging, and it's very difficult to find anyone."[71]

Bilbo answered, "I should think so—in these parts! We are plain quiet folk and have no use for adventures. Nasty disturbing uncomfortable things! Make you late for dinner!"

My journey to be freed from the fear of rejection could only mean one thing: I was going to have to face that dragon. Of course, I only figured that out when I was in the middle of being rejected.

It was nasty, disturbing and uncomfortable. BUT rejection's fiery breath didn't kill me. And, truth be told, I wasn't rejected for very long.

But I will meet that dragon again if I continue on this path. Gandalf told Bilbo, "It does not do to leave a live dragon out of your calculations if you live near him."

Dragons of rejection live in our neighbourhoods and have lairs in most homes and churches. Jaws open and dogmatic flames fly out, should we dare to disagree.

It takes courage to stick to what we believe, especially when we're outnumbered. I've seen a few do it. They didn't run away.

---

[71] J.R.R. Tolkien, *The Hobbit*

They held their ground and kept on loving those who disagreed with them. And their community grew around them and flourished. It became more diverse and more loving.

Now God is asking me to be as brave as Bilbo. Remember, "So comes snow after fire, and even dragons have their endings."

What then shall we say to these things?
If God is for us, who can be against us?
—Romans 8:31 (ESV)

FACES

EVERY TIME I looked up from the pulpit to give an illustration or make a point, I would notice the expressions on people's faces. What were they telling me?

A smiling face says, "Preach it, sister!" An intent look says, "I'm with you." But a furrowed brow might say, "I don't think so" or "You lost me there." What about someone who has their head in their hands? That can't be good. A blank look might mean they're distracted or bored. Then there's a half-smile that says, "Yup, that's the same outfit she wore last time."

My brain takes this in in nanoseconds and files it at the back of my mind for later. If I dared to think about it while I'm preaching, I'd be done for. I get unnerved by blank or troubled faces. So I look for enthusiastic listeners. Their faces encourage me and give me energy.

But, on this new adventure with Jesus, I realize that I don't need them to tell me I'm okay.

Later, when I sat with him and thought about all those faces, I remembered what David said in Psalm 27:8. "My heart says of you, 'Seek his face!' Your face, Lord, I will seek."

Isn't my heart telling me the same thing? Jesus is inviting me to look for his face in the crowd. He wants me to be anchored in him instead of being buoyed by a smile or swamped by a frown.

Yes, my heart sings, "My soul is at rest in God alone. My salvation comes from God."[72]

---

[72] "My Soul Is at Rest" by the Taizé Community from Psalm 62:1

As for me, I will be vindicated
and will see your face;
when I awake,
I will be satisfied with seeing your likeness.
—Psalm 17:15

BLESSED MISTAKES

I'M A LIST maker. When we go camping, I have a list of everything we need categorized and updated yearly. I live by the old boy scout motto "Be prepared." I value efficiency and love it when everything goes smoothly. I'm forever whittling down the possibility of mistakes.

On our way back from a recent camping trip in Washington State, we heard on the radio that the expected wait time to cross the border was an hour. We groaned and decided to have dinner out, hoping the wait time would lessen. But while we dined, it doubled. Double groan. We sat for a long time inching toward Canada. As we did, I wished I had not booked a directee for a spiritual direction session the next morning. Then we could have camped that night and crossed more quickly in the morning.

The next day I went to my office at the church to meet with my directee. The person didn't come. I looked back at the email conversation and realized we had never confirmed the appointment.

This kind of thing drives a be-prepared-efficiency-driven-list-maker crazy. But the Holy Spirit had been speaking to me about mistakes. While on vacation, I read about the life of St. John of the Cross. This story stood out.

One feast day the brother cook let a pot of rice boil over and burn. Far from becoming angry, Fray John quietly consoled the brother, "Don't worry, my son; we can have whatever else you've got. Our Lord does not mean us to have rice today."[73]

Instead of fussing or blaming, St. John had a "habit of seeing the hand of God in all things."[74] How life-giving it is to welcome God's direction in everything, even our mistakes.

So, instead of getting angry with myself or the directee, I wondered why God might want me at the church that morning. I was about to leave when one of the guys that attends the Wednesday Lunch Club showed up and tapped on the window.

"Someone *is* here," he said as I opened the window.

"You're lucky. No one's usually in on a Monday."

"Well, I prayed about it and see?"

He needed food and I got him got some from the church's food bank and from the donations we receive from Cobs Bakery and Starbucks. As I did, he told me more about his situation, hopes and frustrations.

I listened and prayed with him.

"Thank you very much," he said. "God answered my prayer."

When I posted this story on my blog, I found an old sketch of a boy scout. At the top, it said BE PREPARED and at the bottom, it said DO A GOOD TURN DAILY.

That's what God was preparing me for.

> *It's about as useless as a screen door on a submarine.*
> *Faith without works, baby*
> *It just ain't happenin'*
> —Rich Mullins[75]

---

[73] John of the Cross, *The Collected Works of St. John of the Cross,*(translated by Kieran Kavanaugh, O.C.D. and Otilio Rodriguez, O.C.D), 32.

[74] Ibid.

[75] Rich Mullins, "Screen Door," *Songs.*

THE VOICE OF LOVE LOVING

I WOKE IN the night feeling condemned for overeating. A voice kept at me, relentlessly inflicting guilt and shame. It blamed me for using my addiction to food as an excuse to sin. It called me a hypocrite. I repented and vowed to change my ways.

That evening I went to Imago Dei. I don't remember the topic of our reflection, but I do know that the convicting episode I experienced the night before wasn't even on my radar. Yet as soon as we entered into silent prayer, the memory returned. When it did, I heard God say, "That voice wasn't mine."

Relief brought tears to my eyes.

A few days later, at a lecture about Ignatian prayer, Father Richard Soo explained how to discern God's voice. He said, "When the enemy convicts me of sin, I feel bad about myself; but when God convicts me of sin, I feel loved."

I let that sink in: when God convicts me of sin, I feel loved.

Sure God wants to release me from my compulsion to overeat but, thankfully, God doesn't have to shame me into it.

In his book, *What Is Ignatian Spirituality?* David Fleming calls God "Love loving."[76] I wonder what Love loving has to say about my overeating? I would listen to that voice.

Let me not run from the love which You offer.
—Soul of Christ [77]

---

[76] David L. Fleming, SJ, "God Is Love Loving", *What Is Ignatian Spirituality?*, 7.
[77] David L. Fleming, SJ, Soul of Christ prayer, *See Appendix A.*

LOVE SPEAKS TO ME ABOUT FOOD

THE VOICE I would listen to spoke to me about my relationship with food.

Before we left on vacation, I found Geneen Roth's book *Women, Food and God* in the library. In it, Roth talks about the guidelines for eating that have transformed her life. Instead of thinking of them as rules, she thinks of them this way: If love could speak to me about food, this is what it would say.

Roth's guidelines urged me to be fully present when I eat, to listen to my body, and to enjoy each mouthful of food with "gusto and pleasure." God was inviting me to eat contemplatively.

That reminded me of SoulStream's commitment to "attentively respond to the Spirit's presence in our daily choices."[78] The Spirit will help me listen to my body and choose what, when, where, how, and how much to eat.

As I tried to eat contemplatively, the Spirit nudged me to consider the questions Roth asks in her book:

- Why do I overeat?
- What feelings am I avoiding?
- Do I wish I were somewhere else?
- Can I love my body?

As God and I walk together with these questions, I feel the discomfort they raise. I resist God's interference in my life.

---

[78] For SoulStream's Values and Commitments go to
    https://soulstream.org/about-soulstream/

But Love stops and waits with me in my resistance. God knows that there are no other roads but this one. This is the road to freedom.

Still you were ever near to me,
You waited for me to see.
Now You guide me with your counsel,
You hold me in your heart.
—Psalm 73:23, 24[79]

---

[79] Nan C. Merrill, *Psalms For Praying: An Invitation to Wholeness*

THAT SWEET MOON LANGUAGE

IN THE PARABLE of the net, Jesus tells his listeners that the kingdom of heaven is like a fisherman that casts his net wide.[80] He collects everything in the sea: fish and sea creatures, tin cans and old boots. "God wants them all," Jesus says, "the good and the bad.[81] We'll sort later." [82]

In the meantime, we're stuck with each other.

Wouldn't life be easier if God would stop every once in a while and sort out the stinkers? Those bad fish keep ruining our lives and messing up the world with greed and violence.

But, no. God keeps casting the net and continues the ban on sorting. God doesn't seem to be in a hurry to toss anyone out of the kingdom.

Love will do what it takes to convince every single person that they are precious to God.

This King of Love draws the net tight, so tight the creatures in the net are forced to look each other in the eye.

What will our enemies see when they look into our eyes? What will we see in theirs?

That love-stricken poet Hafiz knows:

---

[80] Matthew 13:47-52
[81] See Robert Farrar Capon's *The Parables of the Kingdom*, 147.
[82] Matthew 13:24-30

WITH THAT MOON LANGUAGE

Admit something:
Everyone you see, you say to them,
"Love me."
Of course you do not do this out loud;
Otherwise,
Someone would call the cops.
Still though, think about this,
This great pull in us
To connect.
Why not become the one
Who lives with a full moon in each eye
That is always saying,
With that sweet moon
Language,
What every other eye in this world
Is dying to
Hear.
—Hafiz[83]

You and I have been caught in God's net because Jesus has loved us with his sweet moon language. Now he calls us to love others with a full moon in each eye.

Those other fish?

They're in the net for the very same reason.

---

[83] Hafiz, "With that Moon Language," *Love Poems from God; Twelve Voices from the East and West* (translated by Daniel Ladinsky).

SCARLET FEVER

IF YOU LOOK up this post on my blog, you'll find a wedding photo. Fred's the handsome Royal Canadian Mounted Police officer dressed in red serge, and I'm the smiling twenty-two-year-old bride beside him. We met forty years ago in the indigenous community of Bella Bella.

Back then this tiny village, located on the isolated coast of British Columbia, had barely fifteen kilometres of dirt road. Only a handful of outsiders—teachers, doctors, nurses, and RCMP officers—were invited by the Heiltsuk band to live there.

Constable Hizsa liked to tell people that he was stationed in this remote village soon after he suspended an alderman's license for impaired driving, had the mayor's son's car towed, and attended a traffic accident involving the detachment commander's wife. I found myself there after I graduated from nursing school when jobs were scarce in my home province.

I also wanted to broaden my experience of life. And this one-hotel-no-cable-TV island had lots to show me. The Heiltsuk people expressed their joy easily and loved each other generously. However, in 1979 many families on the "reserve" (as it was called then) were sorely affected by years of abuse at the hands of the settlers. The trauma of being sent to residential schools had taken its toll and many who survived had turned to alcohol.

I happened to be on the dock the day Fred arrived by float plane. The other police officers were out on a call, so I was left to show Fred to his quarters. Before we got through the door of his single-wide trailer, we discovered we had a lot in common. We both grew up in Ontario, our parents had emigrated from Europe, and we loved the outdoors. Soon Fred and I were sharing meals, listening to ABBA, and going for long walks on the beach. After work, we talked about the crazy things that had happened that day and tried to make sense of the violence and pain around us.

Meanwhile, the spinster matron watched these developments from her house across the road. She told us afterward that she wondered how long it would be before another one of her nurses succumbed to "scarlet fever."

One moonlit night, Fred and I were walking on the beach. A few stray dogs tagged along. I stepped from rock to rock as each wave lifted the seaweed and washed the ocean up around my sneakers.

Fred took my hand to keep me from slipping. "You're the woman I've been looking for my whole life," he said.

"Who? Me?"

He smiled. There was no one else there except the dogs.

I couldn't believe someone would choose me to love every day for the rest of their life, but someone did. I will always treasure that moment.

When we come to believe that God loves us that much and more, that is a moment God treasures. I can imagine the Trinity smiling every time they talk about it.

> *O give thanks to the Beloved,*
> *and open your hearts to Love.*
> —Psalm 105:1[84]

---

[84] Nan C. Merrill, *Psalms For Praying: An Invitation to Wholeness*

IS CONTEMPLATIVE SPIRITUALITY FOR EVERYONE?

FROM TIME TO time I've been asked if contemplative spirituality is for everyone. Those who ask confess that they find it difficult and unrewarding to sit still. They experience God much more in doing things. "I'm just not wired that way," they admit, hoping I will let them off the contemplative hook.

"Neither am I," I respond. Neither was Henri Nouwen. He wrote a lot about finding God in silence and solitude, yet he had great difficulty sitting still for five minutes.[85]

But Nouwen persisted and so do I because God desires to be truly known in a way that is unlimited by metaphors and images, thoughts and words. "Be still, and know that I am God," the Lord says in Psalm 46:10.

I read this poem in *Celtic Daily Prayer*:

> *There is a contemplative*
> *in all of us,*
> *almost strangled*
> *but still alive,*
> *who craves quiet*
> *enjoyment of the Now,*
> *and longs to touch*
> *the seamless*
> *garment of silence*
> *which makes whole.*[86]

---

[85] Michael Ford, *Wounded Prophet: A Portrait of Henri J.M. Nouwen* (1999), 5.
[86] Alan P. Tory in *Celtic Daily Prayer* by Northumbria Community.

Whether we are aware of it or not, we all long to be with God alone without any props. The Bible talks about it. Christian mystics remind us of it. Questions open us to it:

Why am I so busy?

Why is work so important to me?

Who am I when I can't do anything?

I want to say all these things to my arms-crossed inquirers, but God doesn't. Love will awaken that deep desire in its time.

You, God, are my God,
earnestly I seek you;
I thirst for you,
my whole being longs for you,
in a dry and parched land
where there is no water.
—Psalm 63:1

WALKING WITH JESUS

I'VE BEEN BEGINNING my day with the *Pray as You Go* app. In these short on-line reflections, I am often asked to imagine myself with Jesus and interact with him.

One morning I was one of the women who followed Jesus.[87] When I got close to him, I waited for him to speak, but he didn't say anything. He just took my hand in his and we walked on.

I returned to that image during a prayer retreat a few days later. In the silence, I pictured myself walking hand in hand with Jesus again. I wondered what might unfold in my imagination when all of a sudden Jesus squeezed my hand as Fred does sometimes. It means: Stop. Look.

There was a deer in the bushes. She grazed so unafraid; did she even notice us? At that moment she stopped chewing and looked at us. A sense of holiness rippled through me.

After the deer went on her way, Jesus and I resumed walking. Where were we going? I felt that stop-look squeeze again. A friend was coming toward us. Groan. I didn't feel like talking to anyone.

Jesus let go of my hand and stepped in front of me so that I was hidden behind him.

"Hey, how's it going?" Jesus began a conversation that kept the person from noticing my presence. I listened and waited for the conversation to end, but it went on for some time. As it did, I leaned my head against Jesus' back and listened to the "Uh-huhs"

---

[87] Mark 5:25-34

reverberate in his chest. His compassion made my heart soften toward this person, but I felt no compunction to be sociable.

After the friend went on, Jesus took my hand again. Again, I wondered where we were going.

Then I realized: it didn't matter.

Jesus, with you by my side enough has been given.
—David L. Fleming, S.J.[88]

---

[88] David L. Fleming, SJ, Soul of Christ prayer, *See Appendix A.*

THE HAND THAT STILLED THE STORM

LATELY, JESUS HAS been inviting me to hold his hand as we walk through life together. That reminds me of something that happened when Heidi was born. She was delivered as planned by caesarean section a week before her due date.

Since I had been working as a nurse in the hospital where she was being delivered, I knew all the medical staff and got to hand-pick some key players who would be in the operating room. The anaesthetist I chose to give me the epidural was especially proficient but had a rather cold bed-side manner.

April 18, 1985, I lay on the operating room table draped and prepped with antiseptic. As soon as the anaesthetist determined I had no feeling in the lower part of my body, the surgeon made the incision. A few minutes later, the general practitioner brought Heidi into the world, joyfully announcing, "It's a girl!"

A girl! I heard her beautiful cry and imagined her wet, wrinkly body. Then the nurse let me see Heidi all wrapped up and perfect. Then she was taken out to Fred, who was anxiously waiting in the hall.

Meanwhile, I was stuck in the operating room with an intravenous tube in one arm, a blood pressure cuff around the other, and the surgical team hovering over the open wound in my abdomen. The tedious process of closing me up and the drugs in my body made me restless. I wanted to turn onto my side but knew I couldn't. A tempest of jittery energy was trapped in my body.

I knew that if someone held my hand, I'd be okay. But who would do that? The doctors and nurses were busy. The one hand available belonged to the anaesthetist who sat idly by watching the drip.

No. Not him.

But the restlessness wouldn't abate. I looked up and said, "Would you hold my hand?"

He looked back quizzically. "Why?"

Before I could come up with an answer, the anaesthetist found my hand and clumsily held it in his. As soon as he did, a wave of calm rolled down my arm and stilled the churning in my body.

Peace returned.

I think about that memory and wonder why Jesus has brought it to mind.

What new birth are you bracing me for, God? What needs settling? I ask as I nervously reach for the hand that stilled the storm.

He got up, rebuked the wind and said to the waves,
"Quiet! Be still!"
Then the wind died down and it was completely calm.
—Mark 4:39

THAT WHICH IS LOST WITHIN ME

ON OCTOBER 5, 2014, an announcement was made to the congregation that my employment at New Life Community Church would end on December 31.

Nervous about the reaction to the coming change, I reached for the hand that stilled the storm.

Often I'm unaware of the storms in my life. Thankfully, God isn't. My Creator has the advantage of being both far and near. From above, the Spirit views where I've been and where I'm heading. Up close, the Spirit sees, feels, and hears what's going on inside me. God has noticed the long hours I've been putting in, how I've neglected my bicycle, Gracie, and how often I comfort myself with food.

At the SoulStream Partners' Retreat in June, I chatted with friends I hadn't seen in a while. When they asked about my life, I told them I would be co-facilitating Living from the Heart, SoulStream's spiritual formation course, and that I'd been trained to direct those praying the Ignatian Spiritual Exercises in Daily Life and hoped to accompany a couple of people through them.

"Yes. I'm still working at the church half-time," I explained. "And, oh yeah, I launched a blog last summer. I post a story or reflection every Friday." After hearing what I'd been up to, people commented that I was doing a lot.

"Are you hearing that?" the Spirit seemed to say.

I thought about my three vocations: writing, spiritual direction, and pastoring. Olympian Eric Liddell once said that he felt God's pleasure when he ran. I feel God's pleasure when I write or accompany someone in spiritual direction. But these endeavours often get pushed to the side. My third occupation, providing leadership in a church, demands most of my time and energy. It also pays the bills.

Sunday morning, as the retreat came to a close, we gathered for worship. John Kiemele, our director, read a poem. He invited us to listen for the line in the poem that shimmered to us.

These words brought tears to my eyes: "The risen, living Christ … seeks for that which is lost within me."

I knew what was lost within me: the "me" that I am on vacation and don't have to be a pastor. The risen Christ wanted to lift the heavy cloak of responsibility from my shoulders. He was whispering, *Go. Be free.* Not just of my fear of rejection but of work I no longer need to do.

Over the next few months, I imagined what it would be like not to be rushed all the time. I longed for a generous amount of time to rest, write, and ride my bike. By the end of the summer, Fred and I were certain that it was time for me to step down as associate pastor of New Life.

When I talked about it with the elders, they confirmed my decision in a practical way: the church didn't have the financial resources to keep me on staff.

It's not easy to leave church work that I love or the paycheck that comes with it. But I can't do it all without getting lost in a din of activity. Jesus sought for me in the successive storms of busyness and lifted his hand.

THE RISEN, LIVING CHRIST

The risen, living Christ
calls me by my name;
comes to the loneliness within me;
heals that which is wounded in me;
comforts that which grieves in me;
seeks for that which is lost within me;
releases me from that which has dominion over me;
cleanses me of that which does not belong to me;
renews that which feels drained within me;
awakens that which is asleep in me;
names that which is formless within me;
empowers that which is newborn within me;
consecrates and guides that which is strong within me;
restores me to this world which needs me;
reaches out in endless love to others through me.
   —Flora Slosson Wuellner [89]

---

[89] Flora Slosson Wuellner, *"The Risen, Living Christ"*
from *Prayer, Fear, and Our Powers*, Upper Room Books.

JUST BE STILL

"BE STILL, AND know that I am God," says the psalmist.[90]

Nearly every Thursday evening, our Imago Dei group gathers to do just that. Of course, there is time for fellowship, reflection and songs, but we also pray in silence for twenty minutes.

Over the years, people in the group have commented on how hard it is to sit still and fend off distractions or sleep. (At the end of an evening, we have ribbed one or two friends who nodded off and began to snore.)

As difficult as it is to practice this type of prayer, no one has ever suggested that we give it up. I think it's because each of us longs to fully know and fully love God directly, without needing the mediation of words, images, or feelings. The Spirit has awakened in us "a naked intent toward God."[91] We long to rest in God alone and commune with our Creator in the core of our being. That communing transforms us.

It's not easy for most people to wrap their minds around the idea that they can be transformed simply by resting. We often assume that personal growth only happens as a result of hard work and determination.

But, think about it. What happened after you were conceived? For nine months you did nothing to make yourself grow. All you did was rest and receive nourishment and loving caresses. Or think of how your body is refreshed between falling

---

[90] Psalm 46:10
[91] *The Cloud of Unknowing,* (edited by William Johnston), 49.

asleep at night and waking up in the morning. Immeasurably more than we can imagine happens when we rest in God.

The author of *The Cloud of Unknowing* says,

> *You will seem to know nothing and to feel nothing except a naked intent toward God in the depths of your being. Try as you might, this darkness and this cloud will remain between you and your God. You will feel frustrated, for your mind will be unable to grasp him, and your heart will not relish the delight of his love. But learn to be at home in this darkness. Return to it as often as you can, letting your spirit cry out to him in love. For if, in this life, you hope to feel and see God as he is in himself, it must be within this darkness and this cloud. But if you strive to fix your love on him forgetting all else, which is the work of contemplation I have urged you to begin, I am confident that God in his goodness will bring you to a deep experience of himself.* [92]

And that, my friends agree, is worth sitting still for.

God can do anything, you know —far more than you could ever imagine or guess or request in your wildest dreams! God does it not by pushing us around but by working within us, God's Spirit deeply and gently within us.
—Ephesians 3:20 (The Message)

---

[92] *The Cloud of Unknowing,* (edited by William Johnston), 49.

NIGHT CROSSING

THIS HAPPENED OVER twenty-five years ago, yet I remember it as if it were yesterday.[93]

"Imagine you are in your favourite place," the instructions for the prayer read. "Perhaps it's on a beach or in a cozy cabin. What do you see, hear, feel, taste, and smell? Are you alone or with others? After you've relaxed there for a while, picture Jesus entering the scene. Let the Holy Spirit take it from there and see what unfolds."

I put down my cup of tea and sat cross-legged on the couch in the afternoon sun. Heidi was napping in her crib and Rudy at kindergarten.

I closed my eyes and pictured myself at the bow of Kimmeridge, the twenty-seven foot sailboat we used to own. Fred was at the helm and our little ones asleep. The gentle winds filled the mainsail and jib. The night sky was clear and the salt air cool. I zipped up my fleece and rested my forearms on the lifelines. My bare feet dangled over the side not far from the water. The only sounds came from the slosh of the waves and ting-ting of the rigging.

I was alone and then I wasn't. Jesus, looking like he did in the pictures with long hair and a white robe, sat right beside me.

I swallowed, took a deep breath and said, "Hi."

"Hello," he said. "Nice night."

"Yes, it is."

---

[93] This story was originally published on my blog at this point. I also included it in *Stories of an Everyday Pilgrim*.

This was my big chance. I could ask Jesus anything. I looked up at the Big Dipper and the pockmarked moon. I remembered that Jesus was with God in the beginning and that through him all things were created.

"What were you thinking about when you made the moon and the stars?" I asked.

"What was I thinking about?" Jesus turned to face me. "I was thinking of the night you and I would be sitting here together looking at them."

My heart thumped in my throat and a tear slid down my cheek. I never guessed he was going to say that.

When I opened my eyes, the world was as it was before. My tea was still warm and Heidi still asleep. Would she notice when she woke up? And when I picked up Rudy from school or welcomed Fred home from work, would they see that I was not the same person I was when they left?

On the wings of the wind, You did come.
—Psalm 18:10[94]

---

[94] Nan C. Merrill, *Psalms For Praying: An Invitation to Wholeness*

EIGHT WEEKS TO THE PROMISED LAND

ARE YOU WONDERING how I am doing since the big announcement? I too wondered how I would fare in the sea of responses. I kept waiting for a wave to broadside me. Would someone be angry with me? Would others be relieved that I was stepping down?

But it's gone smoothly. Many people express their appreciation for what I've done for them personally and for our church. Some kindly ask how Fred and I will make ends meet. Others are inspired by my willingness to follow God's call to be less busy.

But I haven't slowed down yet. In fact, the pace has picked up. I long for the solitude and leisure that is eight weeks away and get anxious thinking about all that needs to be done before then. My prayer times are rushed and unfocused. I pray in the cracks. Deadlines have me trapped and feeling like the Israelites caught between Pharaoh's army and the Red Sea. I need the outrageous faith Moses had. He believed: *God loves us. God is here. God will act.* And God did.

But Moses wasn't always so confident. Like me, he got overwhelmed by all he was expected to do.

Moses said to the Lord, "See, you have said to me, 'Bring up this people'; but you have not let me know whom you will send with me . . . Now if I have found favor in your sight, show me

your ways, so that I may know you and find favor in your
sight. Consider too that this nation is your people." He said,
"My presence will go with you, and I will give you rest."[95]

I complained too and God parted the sea that threatened to separate us: just in time, I was given these verses from Exodus and this poem. They gave me the confidence to continue on toward the Promised Land.

JUST SIT THERE RIGHT NOW

Just
Sit there right now.
Don't do a thing. Just rest.

For your
Separation from God
Is the hardest work in this world.

Let me bring you trays of food and something
That you like to
Drink.

You can use my soft words
As a cushion
For your
Head.
—Hafiz[96]

[95] Exodus 33:12-14
[96] Hafiz, "Just Sit There Right Now," *Love Poems from God; Twelve Voices from the East and West* (translated by Daniel Ladinsky).

GOD PRESENT AS PROMISED

DURING A RESTLESS night, I felt like the Israelites again. All the things I have to do were advancing toward me with their sharp spears, while my heels backed into the Red Sea. The cold reality of deadlines lapped at my ankles.

Help God, I prayed again. Remember you promised to be with me.

I longed to be settled to sleep, but more worries came out of hiding.

Sometime in the night, I remembered what a friend said. "I just want to go with God's flow. Not forcing it, not holding back." Her words, inspired by a poem by Rainer Maria Rilke, reminded me that I don't have to make anything happen. God is present, as promised and flowing in me like a river. When I feel myself pushing to make something work, I don't need to push harder. I need to let go and relax back into the flow.

In the morning, I found the poem my friend quoted and let this part speak to my soul.

May what I do flow from me like a river,
no forcing and no holding back,
the way it is with children.

Then in these swelling and ebbing currents,
these deepening tides moving out, returning,
I will sing you as no one ever has,

streaming through widening channels
into the open sea.[97]

I'm drawn to the image of singing—not fretting, not panicking, but singing—in the swelling and ebbing currents and deepening tides.

As I sit in an eddy of God's presence, I feel anxiety ebb and hope begins to swell. I am being drawn into a current of faith: God loves me. God is here. God will act.

---

[97] Rainer Maria Rilke, *Rilke's Book of Hours: Love Poems to God* (translated by Anita Barrows and Joanna Macy).

ON THIS MOUNTAIN

LAST WEEK I talked about deadlines closing in on me. One of them was SoulStream's Living from the Heart course. It would be my first time co-facilitating a six-day intensive in spiritual formation, and I wanted to prepare well for it. Shortly before I left to go on the course, which was held on Sumas Mountain near Abbotsford, I happened to read these verses:

> *On this mountain, the Lord Almighty will prepare*
> *a feast of rich food for all peoples,*
> *a banquet of aged wine—*
> *the best of meats and the finest of wines.*
> *On this mountain, he will destroy*
> *the shroud that enfolds all peoples,*
> *the sheet that covers all nations;*
> *he will swallow up death forever.*[98]

As I read about the feast and fine wines that would be enjoyed on "this mountain," I sensed God elbowing me in the ribs and winking at me. We were going to be on a mountain where Peggy and Pat, the hosts of Twin Creeks Lodge, would serve up a feast at every meal. There would be good wine, too, at our midweek Sabbath celebration. God seemed to be saying that, during our intensive, the Holy Spirit would wipe away tears,

---

[98] Isaiah 25:6-8

remove shame and swallow up death. On this mountain, we would be glad we trusted God.

And we were. I was one of three facilitators that led the participants in prayers, teachings and activities. Yet we were often aware of a fourth: the Holy Spirit.

During a silent pause, the wind rustled the leaves right on cue. Words in our prayers, chosen weeks before, matched our experience in ways we hadn't anticipated. Bravery was given, honest words spoken, bruised reeds protected, and smoldering wicks shielded.[99] With unveiled faces we beheld God's glory as we listened to our lives and listened again to God speaking in them.[100] Each person that came to the mountain was enlivened in one way or another.

My spirit soared when a Voice spoke to me:
"Come, come to the Heart of Love!"
How long I have stood within the house of fear
yearning to enter the gates of Love!
—Psalm 122: 1, 2 [101]

---

[99] Isaiah 42:3
[100] 2 Corinthians 3:18
[101] Nan C. Merrill, *Psalms For Praying: An Invitation to Wholeness*

Advent I 2014

WAITING

WHAT IF THE one you're waiting for never comes?

It was only choir practice.

I was thirteen years old and proud to be the youngest member of the choir at Wellburn United Church. Every Thursday at seven forty-five, after our neighbours had milked their cows and changed their clothes, they would pull into our driveway to give me a ride to the church, a kilometre away.

One winter evening, at seven-forty, I got ready and waited in the kitchen. Ten minutes later I was overheating and took off my toque and mitts. Five minutes after that, I needed to go to the bathroom but didn't dare leave my post. We would be late now and they'd be in a hurry when they arrived.

At eight o'clock a car drove by in the opposite direction. I watched the red tail lights disappear down the gravel road.

At eight-fifteen I took off my coat and boots and headed upstairs to my room.

"I thought you were going to the church," my dad said.

"My ride didn't come," I replied. "I guess they forgot about me."

I must not be that important, I thought and added that thought to all the other evidence I'd collected that proved I didn't matter.

For years after that Thursday night, waiting for anyone made me nervous.

This Sunday a whole season of waiting begins, yet I am thrilled. I know the One I'm waiting for will come. He always does.

For hundreds of years, Israel waited for their Messiah. Finally, he came. The angel Gabriel announced the good news to a teenager named Mary. She became pregnant by the Holy Spirit and gave birth to the Saviour of the world in Bethlehem, just as the prophets said.

Jesus came to earth because we matter. His Spirit remains with us now because we always will.

> *The people walking in darkness*
> *have seen a great light;*
> *on those living in the land of deep darkness*
> *a light has dawned...*
> *For to us a child is born,*
> *to us a son is given,*
> *and the government will be on his shoulders.*
> *And he will be called*
> *Wonderful Counselor, Mighty God,*
> *Everlasting Father, Prince of Peace.*
> —Isaiah 9:2, 6

Advent II 2014

A WONDROUS THOUGHT

AFTER THE ANGEL Gabriel's visit, Mary woke to a new reality.[102]

The pondering of her heart emerged on her lips as she washed the dishes and passed by the beggars on her way to fetch water.

"My soul glorifies the Lord," she sang to herself. "He has filled the hungry with good things and sent the rich away. From now on all generations will call me blessed, for the Mighty One has done great things for me." The Saviour is in me! What a wondrous thought.

But weeks passed and nothing changed. Mary began to wonder if it had all been a dream until one morning a wave of nausea propelled her out of bed just in time. She threw up in the garden and then leaned against the clay brick wall wiping her mouth with the back of her hand as perspiration cooled her brow.

It happened the next day and the next. Mary hadn't dreamt it; she was pregnant with God's Son. That first Advent, Mary wasn't waiting for Christ to come. He was already there, her growing belly a testimony.

In our Advent we, like Israel, cry, "How long, O Lord? Will you forget us forever? How long will you hide your face from us?"[103] We keep looking for God to come in power and fill the hungry with good things. Meanwhile, the Holy Spirit has already overshadowed us, seeding Christ in us.

---

[102] Luke 1: 26-38, 43, 48, 49, 53
[103] Psalm 13:1

Now it is God who is waiting for us. God waits for us to awaken to the wondrous thought that Christ is in us, with us, and for us.

We are being filled full of God.[104]

KEEPING WATCH

In the morning
When I began to wake,
It happened again—

That feeling
That You, Beloved,
Had stood over me all night
Keeping watch,

That feeling
That as soon as I began to stir
You put Your lips on my forehead
And lit a Holy Lamp
Inside my Heart.
—Hafiz[105]

---

[104] Ephesians 3:19
[105] Hafiz, "Keeping Watch," *I Heard God Laughing: Poems of Hope and Joy* (translated by Daniel Ladinsky).

Advent III 2014

AWARENESS

THIS ADVENT, I'VE been living into the wondrous thought that Christ is in me, with me and for me. I noticed that whenever I undertook a task or wrote a blog post, I wasn't alone. My Divine Friend was there, helping me find the wisdom or words I needed.

Recognizing God's presence in those simple activities ignited a flicker of joy in my chest. That joy made me stop and breathe in the awareness that I am in Christ, and he is in me.

The image of myself as a leaky bucket in God's ocean of love came to mind. I heard, *All you long for, you already have.*

The part of me that focuses on my cracks reacted to that thought. I could provide a list of things I long for but don't have—not possessions per se but virtues. I wish I wasn't so self-preoccupied, for example.

But the part of me that focuses on God's love, flowing in and out of my cracks, smiled. Love is transforming me.

In *Presence and Encounter,* David Benner says that awareness of God's presence "creates space and openness that allow us to be present to more than our usual self-preoccupations."

Awareness quiets the self-serving chatter in my head and frees me to hear something new. And I did.

Eventually I realized that focusing on my cracks *is* self-preoccupation, and I watched it float away.

> *If anyone is in Christ, that person is a new creation.*
> *The old has gone, the new is here!*
> *—2 Corinthians 5:17*

Advent IV 2014

ENCOUNTERING GOD IN OUR EMOTIONS

THE CHRISTMAS SEASON tends to evoke a range of emotions in us. While we express tidings of comfort and joy, we may feel anything but comforted or joyful. It's good to pay attention to those unsettling feelings and listen to what they're saying.

"Why would I want to do that?" you may ask. "Won't that get me into trouble or make me feel worse?"

Perhaps you've seen the train image in Campus Crusade's *Four Spiritual Laws*. FACT is the engine, FAITH is the coal car; and FEELING, the caboose. The point of the illustration is that Christians need to rely on the truth of God's Word to guide them no matter what they're feeling.

We know from life experience that we don't want to let our feelings drive the train. However, we have to stop uncoupling them from our lives. Our emotions, even the unpleasant ones, are holy ground. We can encounter God in them.

To do that, we must first become aware of God's presence. St. Theophan the Recluse, a nineteenth-century Russian Orthodox priest, said, "To pray is to descend with the mind into the heart and there to stand before the face of the Lord, ever-present, all-seeing, within you."[106]

So begin there. With your mind, imagine yourself meeting Christ in the core of your being. Stand before him. Look at him looking at you with love.

---

[106] Richard J. Foster, *Sanctuary of the Soul: Journey into Meditative Prayer*, 35.

In his loving presence, tell Jesus about the event that incited the strong feeling you experience. It may help to picture the emotion as an angry cat, hair-raised and pacing. Now name the feeling. For example, it could be jealousy or loneliness. Don't judge it or analyze it. Just let it hiss and meow there with you and Jesus.

When there is a bit of space between you and your feeling, ask it what it wants to tell you. You may hear something like "I feel invisible when other people get the attention I crave" or "There's something wrong with me; that's why I'm alone."

Watch how Jesus responds when he hears what your feelings say. Notice his compassion. What does he do and say next? Underneath your words is a longing that Jesus wants to fill.

Once you've been with Jesus there, you'll find your feisty feeling curled up in your lap, as harmless as a kitten. And you, having encountered the living God, will be transformed.

Where can I go from your Spirit?
Where can I flee from your presence?
If I go up to the heavens, you are there;
if I make my bed in the depths, you are there.
—Psalm 139: 7, 8

EMMANUEL

when Jesus came
he didn't sneak in
through the back door
of poverty selling
magic tricks for
applause

no

Jesus came poor
entered every day
of every life
and never
left

MYSTERY AND MAGIC

MIDNIGHT MARKS THE end of 2014 as well as the end of my nine years as associate pastor of New Life Community Church. I spent the day emptying my desk and hanging out with the Wednesday Lunch Club. Tonight Fred and I will ring in the New Year with good friends. Next week we head down to the Oregon coast for five days of beach walking, reading and relaxing.

God has brought my story to a satisfying conclusion. The New Life community has expressed their appreciation to me in notes, gifts, speeches, hugs and tears. Like any good writer, God has carefully tied up the loose ends of this novel and is preparing a new storyboard.

I'm at home writing this in my newly renovated study where I will offer spiritual direction. The walls are sage coloured (thanks to Fred for painting it) and the dominant piece of art is called *Dreaming Tree in the Field of Magic* by Melissa Graves-Brown. I wonder what magic will be woven into the new story God is writing.

> *When we walk to the edge of all the light we have*
> *and take that first step into the darkness of the unknown,*
> *we must believe one of two things will happen:*
>
> *There will be something solid for us to stand on,*
> *or, we will be taught how to fly.*
> —Patrick Overton[107]

---

[107] Patrick Overton, *The Leaning Tree*, 1975, p.78.

Blessed are those whose strength is in you,
whose hearts are set on pilgrimage.
—Psalm 84:5

APPENDIX A:
SOULSTREAM COMMUNITY'S
DAILY PRAYERS

MORNING PRAYER
—Karen Webber

Blessed Trinity
I receive your love,
your presence,
and this day as a gift from you.
I open my heart to you.
Please lead me deeper
into your transforming love
as we live these next hours together.
Amen.

NOON PRAYER
—Rob Peterson

Lord, we pause at noon from work and activity
to remember the many gifts
that come from Your heart.

Thank You for food and meaningful work.
Thank You for the beauty and rhythm of each day.

Thank You that You lovingly accept us as we are
and invite us to rest in the intimacy of that love.

Guard us, Lord, from seeking to find our identity
in performance or professions.
Keep us awake to Your sustaining love
the remainder of this day.
Grant us the courage to delight in the life that is ours
and may the peace you have given to us
make its way to those You bring across our path.
Amen

NIGHT PRAYER
—Cherie Tetz-Christensen and Jeff Imbach
    (adapted from a prayer by St. Augustine)

Loving God,
as I close my eyes
and say goodnight
to You and all this day has given,
I leave all of what has been
and what will be tomorrow.
in Your protective care.

Hold me, and all that is a part of me, as
I lie here—thankful to be
resting in your presence.

Keep watch, dear God,
with all who work, or watch, or weep this night,
and give Your angels charge over those who sleep.

Tend the sick,
give rest to the weary,
bless the dying,
soothe the suffering,

stand with the oppressed,
shield the joyous;
and all for your love's sake!
Amen.

SOUL OF CHRIST
—David Fleming, SJ

Jesus, may all that is you flow into me.
May your body and blood
be my food and drink.
May your passion and death
be my strength and life.
Jesus, with you by my side
enough has been given.
May the shelter I seek
be the shadow of your cross.
Let me not run from the love which you offer,
But hold me safe from the forces of evil.
On each of my dyings
shed your light and your love.
Keep calling to me
until that day comes when with your saints,
I may praise you forever.

APPENDIX B:
PRAYER RETREAT OUTLINES

FOR A NUMBER of years, the Tri-Cities Imago Dei group has been having one-day prayer retreats that are simple, wonderful and free. We bring our own lunch. The group member who hosts provides tea and coffee.

Format:

10:00 am:	Gather for fellowship over tea or coffee
10:30 am:	Silence, light the Christ Candle
	Begin with an opening prayer
	Share a reflection
	Review prayer retreat outline/plan for the day
11:00 am	Silent prayer, reflection, walk, journal, rest, have lunch
3:00 pm:	Gather together to share and pray for each other
4:00 pm:	Closing prayer

In the first half hour, the day's facilitator (one of the people attending) shares with the group a scripture passage as well as a reflective reading, song, poem or picture and some reflective questions. Then we disperse into different rooms or nooks in the house while maintaining silence.

During the four hours of silence, we take walks, knit, journal and, of course, pray. Using cell phones, the internet or reading (even spiritual books) is discouraged.

For the last hour of the retreat, we gather together and share one or two things that arose that were significant to us. After each person has shared, we hold them up to God in silence before moving on to the next person.

Guidelines for sharing:
- Sharing is optional.
- Receive what is offered as a gift.
- No commenting, advice-giving or fixing.
- Keep what has been shared in confidence.

See also: Circle of Trust Touchstones for Safe and Trustworthy Space
http://www.couragerenewal.org/touchstones/

I have included five prayer retreat outlines prepared by members of our Imago Dei group. More outlines are available on my blog under "Resources."

WHAT GOD HAS GIVEN, WHAT GOD IS DOING

—Esther Hizsa

BEGIN YOUR TIME together with this reading:

God can get tiny if we're not careful. I'm certain we all have an image of God that becomes the touchstone, the controlling principle, to which we return when we stray.

My touchstone image of God comes by way of my friend and spiritual director, Bill Cain, S.J. Years ago he took a break from his own ministry to care for his father as he died of cancer. His father had become a frail man, dependent on Bill to do everything for him. Though he was physically not what he had been, and the disease was wasting him away, his mind remained alert and lively. In the role reversal common to adult children who care for their dying parents, Bill would put his father to bed and then read him to sleep, exactly as his father had done for him in childhood. Bill would read from some novel, and his father would lie there staring at his son smiling.

Bill was exhausted from the day's care and work and would plead with his dad, "Look, here's the idea. I read to you, you fall asleep." Bill's father would impishly apologize and dutifully close his eyes. But this wouldn't last long. Soon enough, Bill's father would pop one eye open and smile at his son.

Bill would catch him and whine, "Now, come on." The father would again oblige, until he couldn't anymore, and the other eye would open to catch a glimpse of his son. This went on and on and after his father's death, Bill knew that this evening ritual was really a story of a father who just couldn't take his eyes off his kid. How much more so God. Anthony de Mello writes, "Behold the One beholding you, and smiling."

God would seem to be too occupied in being unable to take Her eyes off us to spend any time raising an eyebrow in disapproval. What's true of Jesus is true for us, and so this voice breaks through the clouds and comes straight at us. "You are my Beloved, in whom I am wonderfully pleased." There is not much "tiny" in that.[108]

Love invites us to receive good gifts:

Jesus said, "Don't bargain with God. Be direct. Ask for what you need. This isn't a cat-and-mouse, hide-and-seek game we're in. If your child asks for bread, do you trick him with sawdust? If he asks for fish, do you scare him with a live snake on his plate? As bad as you are, you wouldn't think of such a thing. You're at least decent to your own children. So don't you think the God who conceived you in love will be even better?" —Matthew 7:7-11 (The Message)

---

[108] Gregory Boyle, SJ., *Tattoos on the Heart: The Power of Boundless Compassion*, 19.

Love invites us to give our entire attention to what God is doing right now:

> *Jesus said, "If God gives such attention to the appearance of wildflowers—most of which are never even seen—don't you think he'll attend to you, take pride in you, do his best for you? What I'm trying to do here is to get you to relax, to not be so preoccupied with getting, so you can respond to God's giving. People who don't know God and the way he works fuss over these things, but you know both God and how he works. Steep your life in God-reality, God-initiative, God-provisions. Don't worry about missing out. You'll find all your everyday human concerns will be met.*
>
> *"Give your entire attention to what God is doing right now, and don't get worked up about what may or may not happen tomorrow. God will help you deal with whatever hard things come up when the time comes."*
> —Matthew 6:30-34 (The Message)

For reflection and prayer:

God is not tiny, but God can become tiny enough to enter a life cracked open a little. Will you allow God to enter into your mind and heart? And, once in, will you allow God to show you a love as big as the universe, as tender as a new mother, as playful as Bill Cain's father?

- What gift has God given you recently? How did it make you feel when you received it? How do you feel when you think about it now? What does that gift tell you about God?
- Why now? Why has God given you this gift at this particular time in your life?
- Is there something else God would like you to notice as you sit with this gift?

- What is God inviting you to do with what has been given or unfolded?
- How would you like to express your gratitude to God who "can't keep Her eyes off you"?

> *i thank You God for most this amazing*
> *day: for the leaping greenly spirits of trees*
> *and a blue true dream of sky; and for everything*
> *which is natural which is infinite which is yes*
>
> *(i who have died am alive again today,*
> *and this is the sun's birthday; this is the birth*
> *day of life and of love and wings: and of the gay*
> *great happening illimitably earth)*
>
> *how should tasting touching hearing seeing*
> *breathing any—lifted from the no*
> *of all nothing—human merely being*
> *doubt unimaginable You?*
>
> *(now the ears of my ears awake and*
> *now the eyes of my eyes are opened)*
> —e.e. cummings

GOD IS LOVE LOVING

—Esther Hizsa

BEGIN THIS RETREAT by sharing loving images of God. You may use artwork or a story like this one:

> In a sermon, Pastor Lance Odegard of Artisan Church in Vancouver told this story. Lance's son was caught doing something wrong and sent him to his room. Lance went to talk with him and as soon as he took his son onto his lap, the boy began to cry. His shoulders were going up and down like jackhammers, and he could hardly speak. "I . . . I . . . f-f-feel so g-g-guilty," he said. Lance wrapped his arms around his son and started to cry too.
>
> "Dad," his son said. "Why are you crying?"
>
> Lance was at a loss for words for a moment, then replied. "Because you're crying."
>
> After they talked about what happened, the boy said to his father. "Every night you tell me that you love me, now I know how big that love is."[109]

---

[109] Story used with permission.

God Is Love Loving

Ignatius's life changed drastically in 1521. He was a soldier serving the kingdom of Castile, fighting to defend the city of Pamplona against a French attack. During the battle, a cannonball struck him in the legs. Badly injured, Ignatius was taken to his family castle in the town of Loyola to recuperate. There he endured two extremely painful operations to repair his wounds and spent many months convalescing. Ignatius had a lot of time to think about his life, which, to that point, had been an undistinguished and unsatisfying pursuit of military glory and frivolous pastimes.

Ignatius was a keenly observant man. His talent for simple "noticing" or "taking note" became a cornerstone of his approach to the spiritual life. In 1521, bored and restless as he healed in his family's home, Ignatius took special notice of the movements in his own spirit.

He had asked for romance novels to read. These tales of love and adventure were the most popular printed books of the time, as they are in our time, and Ignatius loved to fill his imagination with these stories. But the only books available in the house were a life of Christ and a book of stories about saints. Ignatius read these instead, and he was struck by the feelings they stirred in his heart. The stories of Jesus and the heroes of the faith inspired and stimulated him. By contrast, he was restless and discontented when he remembered his favorite tales of romantic love and adventure.

Gradually, a new and inspiring image of God began to form in Ignatius's mind. He saw God as a

God of Love. This was no abstract philosophical concept. God as Love was no longer just a scriptural statement. Ignatius experienced God as an intensely personal, active, generous God, a loving. God creates, and by so doing, God is actively showering us with gifts. God acts, and all God's actions show God's wisdom and love.

God's love is unconditional. It is not something we earn or buy or bargain for. God does not say, "I will love you if you keep my commandments" or "I will love you if you go to Lourdes." Lying on his sickbed—in pain, crippled, agitated—Ignatius came to understand that active loving was God's most outstanding quality. This is his foundational image of God. He arrived at it by "noting" how God dealt with him in his body, soul, and spirit, and through the people and events in his everyday life . . .

This image of God affects how we understand the purpose of our lives. If we think that God loves us only if we act in a certain way, we will see our lives as a time of testing. We need to rise to the challenge, to avoid mistakes, to labor to do the right thing. But if God is Love loving, our life is a time of growing and maturing. "All the things in this world" are ways to become closer to God. Lovers don't test each other. Lovers don't constantly demand that the other measure up. Lovers give to those they love.
    —David L. Fleming[110]

---

[110] David L. Fleming, *What Is Ignatian Spirituality?*, p.7-9.

First Prayer Period

1. *Descend*

> *"Descend with the mind into the heart*
> *and there stand before the face of the Lord,*
> *ever-present, all seeing, within you."*
> —Theophan the Recluse

- Ask Jesus for the grace you need to envision God as Love loving (an active lover attentively loving you), to remain present, and to open to God.
- Be attentive to God and to yourself in the silence (most of the hour).
- As you sit in the silence with God, pay attention to what you notice has been going on in your life. What stands out? What feelings emerge along with them?
- As you continue to sit with God and the event and feelings around it, invite God to do what God wants to do: actively love you.
- Is there something that you have been reading in scripture lately that relates?
- Allow your time with God to be a new landscape, an open vista, in which God takes the lead and interacts with you.

2. *Converse*
- Near the end of the hour take 5 minutes or so to have a conversation with God about what came up in your prayer period.

3. *Journal*
- After your hour of prayer, take time to write down what was significant to you in this prayer period.

Second Prayer Period

Use the same structure as above.

This time, allow the louder emotions and events in your life to take a seat and "let your shy soul speak" (Parker Palmer). As you sit quietly with God, allow a less emotionally charged event or connected events (and accompanying emotion) emerge.

Once again, allow your time with God to be a new landscape, an open vista in which God takes the lead and interacts with you.

AN IGNATIAN PRAYER RETREAT: MEETING JESUS IN SCRIPTURE AND IN DAILY LIFE

—Joy Richardson

OPENING REFLECTION:

Five tight buds, glossy purple lollipops, greeted me as I passed them on my way to morning prayers. Many flowers that I recognized were blooming at Twin Creeks Lodge—iris, geraniums, petunias, pansies, and daisies—but I'd never seen buds like these before. By mid-morning, one had opened up to the sun. "It's a strawflower," Deb told me.

Next morning, there were five buds again. Had I been seeing things? Where was the flower? Before noon the blossom reappeared. It closed at night and opened in the day!

Every time I passed the strawflowers during Living from the Heart course, I looked to see what they were doing. And they, in turn, looked at me and asked, "Are you open or closed?"

During the week-long intensive, Deb Arndt, Jeff Imbach and I introduced the participants to ancient prayer practices and explored contemplative living with them. We watched them open up to God and to one another.

It sounds easier than it is. At times, I was as tight as a bud, anxious that I might say or do something that would inhibit God's work in a participant's life. The strawflower invited me to relax and open myself to the sun. So did morning and evening prayers, the lighting of the Christ candle, the gathering of this little community as we ate, shared and laughed together. Even the rhythm of my breath—full, then empty, then full again—encouraged me to trust that God was at work in me too.

By the end of our time together, spring had ended and summer arrived. The strawflower no longer needed to retreat at night. I long for the day when I will remain open to God and bask in Love's warmth. But for now, I sense, it's enough to listen to the flowers.

—Esther Hizsa[111]

First Prayer Period: Contemplation of Scripture

Allow one hour and fifteen minutes for each prayer period with a ninety-minute break in between to eat, walk, relax, knit, or do whatever does not actively engage your mind.

1. Opening Prayer:
O Lord, I acknowledge that I am in your presence.
I offer this time to you.
Lead my heart and mind.
May everything I feel, think and do be directed purely
toward your greater praise and service. Amen.
—St. Ignatius of Loyola

---

[111] "Questioned by a Strawflower" by Esther Hizsa, *An Everyday Pilgrim* Blog June 12, 2015 and May 19, 2017.

2. Preparation: Choose a scripture passage and read it.
    - Luke 13:10-13 Healing of the Crippled Woman
    - Mark 1:9-11 The Baptism of Jesus

    Visualize the scene: smells, sounds, temperature, surroundings, characters, clothes, tastes, things you touch, etc.

    Ask God for your Heart's Desire (i.e. what you specifically need at this point.) e.g. Ask for a deeply felt awareness of God's love for you.

3. The Prayer of Imagination (main section-45 min.):
    - Be in the scene. Slow down. Wait. There is lots of time.
    - See the characters. Who are you?
    - Listen to what they are saying. How does this impact you?
    - What are they doing? What is your reaction?
    - What are they feeling? What are you feeling?
    - What do you say and/or do in that scene?
    - What do you say to Jesus? What does Jesus say to you?
    - What does Jesus do? What do you do in response?
    - Savour and relish your time with Jesus. Be sure to get "up close and personal"[112] with Jesus. Look in his eyes. Allow him to look into yours. The point of the spiritual life is to know Jesus, not know about him, but to know him.

4. Talk with Jesus (10 min.):
    - Talk about your prayer with Jesus. What was significant to you?

5. Closing prayer

---

[112] Father Richard Soo, SJ

6. Written Prayer Review (15 min.):
  - Move to a different spot.
  - Write down what happened that was particularly significant to you. Include how you felt. This helps you notice what God was doing in your prayer experience.
  - Being in this prayer in three different ways (imagination, talking it over, review), allows your experience of Jesus to deepen. That is extremely important.

Second Prayer Period: Finding God in Our Own Lives

The Old Testament is a love story between God and Israel. The Gospels are a love story between God and the apostles. My story is the love story between God and me. It is where my inner life becomes the source of my matter for prayer.

1. Opening Prayer

2. Preparation: Jesus is with us in the good times and the hard times. This prayer helps us to experience Jesus in a specific moment in our lives. Choose a moment or experience that you are going to bring to the Lord before you start your prayer. Today, choose a time you sensed God's love. It might be a personal encounter with God or a life-defining moment.
  - Visualize the scene in detail.
  - Ask God for your Heart's Desire.

3. The Prayer of Imagination (45 min.):
  - Relive the moment/experience. Don't just remember it or observe it.
  - Enter the scene. See each of the people. Where are you?
  - Look around slowly. What do you see and hear and smell? What are you wearing?

- Where is Jesus? What is he doing? What is he saying? What is he saying to you?
- What are you doing? What are you saying?
- What are you saying to Jesus? What does he say to you in reply?
- Just "be" with Jesus.
- Feel how you felt in the experience.
- Feel: imagine God feeling what you were feeling then.
- Feel what is in God's heart for you, God's love for you. Let it transform you. This is not a time to get a message from God and then do it. What changes us is quality time with Jesus, soaking up his presence.
- Savour and relish your time with Jesus.
- (If sometime you choose a difficult experience, and then imagine what God was feeling as God was feeling your pain.)

4. Talk with Jesus (10 min.):
   - Talk about your prayer with Jesus. What was significant to you?

5. Closing Prayer

6. Written Prayer Review (15 min.): Move to a different spot. Write down what happened and what you felt.

A BASKET FULL OF FRESH BREAD

—Esther Hizsa

OPEN YOUR TIME together with one or more of these:

The mystery of spiritual emptiness
may be living in a pilgrim's heart, and yet
the knowing of it may not be his (or hers) . . .
Wait for the illuminating openness,
as though your chest were filling with Light.
Don't look for it outside yourself.
You are the source of milk. Don't milk others!
There is a milk-fountain inside you . . .
There is a basket of fresh bread on your head,
and yet you go door to door asking for crusts.
Knock on your inner door. No other.
—Rumi[113]

I have learnt to love You late,
beauty at once so ancient and so new!
I have learnt to love You late!
You were within me,
and I was in the world outside myself.
—Augustine, *Confessions*

---

[113] *Rumi: The Book of Love,* (translated by Coleman Barks)

Do you not know that you are a temple of God
and that the Spirit of God dwells in you?
—1 Corinthians 3:16

To them [the saints], God chose to make known
how great among the Gentiles
are the riches of the glory of this mystery,
which is Christ in you, the hope of glory.
—Colossians 1:27

Guard the good deposit that was entrusted to you
—guard it with the help of the Holy Spirit who lives in us.
—2 Timothy 1:14

God is our refuge and strength,
an ever-present help in trouble.
Therefore we will not fear, though the earth give way
and the mountains fall into the heart of the sea,
though its waters roar and foam
and the mountains quake with their surging.

There is a river whose streams make glad the city of God,
the holy place where the Most High dwells.
God is within her, she will not fall;
God will help her at break of day.
Nations are in uproar, kingdoms fall;
God lifts God's voice, the earth melts.

The LORD Almighty is with us;
the God of Jacob is our fortress.
Come and see what the LORD has done,
the desolations God has brought on the earth.

God makes wars cease
to the ends of the earth.
God breaks the bow and shatters the spear;
God burns the shield with fire.
God says, "Be still, and know that I am God;
I will be exalted among the nations,
I will be exalted in the earth."

The LORD Almighty is with us;
the God of Jacob is our fortress.

— Psalm 46: 1-11

For reflection and prayer:

- What words or images were you drawn to in the poems and scriptures above? What do they tell you about yourself and God?

- Knock on your inner door. Peek inside at your own inner landscape? What do you see? Mountains, desert, city, shoreline, countryside, slum? What feelings emerge? What message do those feelings bring? What invitation does God have for you as you welcome and listen to them?

- Consider that your inner landscape is the holy place where the Most High Dwells. Imagine Jesus showing you around his abode. What would he like you to notice? What does he say or do? What does he feel?

- Rest a while inside yourself with God. What has been discovered, treasured, or redeemed?

In Scetis, a brother went to see Abba Moses
and begged him for a word.
The old man said,
"Go and sit in your cell
and your cell will teach you everything."
—A saying from the Desert Fathers

WHEN ISRAEL WAS A CHILD, I LOVED HER

—Joy Richardson

"Our experience of God's love is so great; it trumps our fears, our wants. Everything else pales. This is where we want to go."
—Father Richard Soo, SJ

As YOU BEGIN, ask God for the grace you need. For example:

- to experience God's love for you.
- to listen to what God says.
- to have a generous, committed and open heart and amazement at your existence and at how personally God relates to you.
- that you may grow in freedom to hold on to all that brings you into a deeper relationship with God and let go of all that draws you away from God.

As you pray, turn on your heart.

- Go to where your heart is leading you. Listen.
- Be content to just be in God's presence.
- When you are moved by something, stay there.

"The Spirit helps us in our weakness." —Romans 8:26-27

First Prayer Period:
"When Israel was a child I loved him (her)." —Hosea 11:1-11
(Alternate: Psalm 131, Song of Quiet Trust.)

Process:
- Read the passage.
- Welcome God's Presence. Use Opening Prayer (175) or SoulStream's Morning Prayer (160).
- Pray for a specific grace.
- Meditate on the passage (40-50 minutes).
- Read slowly and prayerfully.
- Listen to yourself, your heart and your own reactions.
- Listen to what might be from God, maybe a picture, memory, song, etc. Then stop. Pause and feel it for as long as possible.
- You don't have to get to the end of the passage again.
- If you still have more time, continue reading until the next you are aware of another feeling. Stop and feel that. Continue.

Have a conversation with Jesus about what took place in your prayer time. (10 min.)

Write a "prayer review." Reflect on your experience of your prayer, your feelings, thoughts and what happened. This helps us notice what God is doing.

Some questions that might help:
- What happened inside me during the period of prayer?
- How did I feel about what went on?
- What was my mood, change in mood? What feelings flowed through me? What thoughts came in and out of my mind? Where was I drawn to dwell?
- How were God and I present or absent to each other?
- Was I praying for anything in particular? What was God's response?[114]

---

[114] J. Veltri, S.J., "The Review of Prayer."

Second Prayer Period:
- Imagine a carefree time with Jesus.
- If you have a favourite spot from when you were a child, go back there. If you don't, choose a place where you would have liked to spend time as a child, e.g. a beach. Go to that place.
- Be a child of 5 or 6 years old. Imagine a time that is carefree, a time before rules and having to do what is right (e.g. only one treat a day). Imagine a time of freedom. This time with Jesus is a loving time of joy and spontaneity. Spend 40-50 minutes with Jesus. Enjoy!

Process:
- Welcome God's Presence (Preparatory Prayer or Morning Prayer)
- Pray for a specific grace.
- Be a child in a place of freedom and joy with Jesus.
- Have a conversation with Jesus.
- Write a prayer review.

Preparing for our sharing time (for groups):
- As you read your first prayer review, allow room for the Holy Spirit to connect with you. Let what you are reading wash over you. Soak in it (like a bath). What is God's flow over you like? Be relaxed. Be open to the unexpected.
- Read your second prayer review in the same way.

BIBLIOGRAPHY

- Augustine, *Confessions* (397 AD)
- Benner, David G. *Surrender to Love* (InterVarsityPress; Downers Grove), 2003.
  ———. *Presence and Encounter: The Sacramental Possibilities of Everyday Life* (Brazos Press; Ada). 2014.
- Bloom, Anthony. *Beginning to Pray* (Paulist Press; New York), *1970*.
- Boyle, SJ. Gregory. *Tattoos on the Heart: The Power of Boundless Compassion* (Simon and Schuster; New York), 2011.
- Buechner, Frederick. *Now and Then: A Memoir of Vocation*, (Harper & Row; San Francisco), 1983.
  ———, *The Sacred Journey*, (Harper & Row; San Francisco), 1982.
- Capon, Robert Farrar, The Parables of the Kingdom, (Eerdmans; Grand Rapids), 2000 (Reprint).
- *The Cloud of Unknowing*, 14th C. anonymous English author, edited by William Johnston, (Doubleday; New York), 1973.
- Fleming, David L. SJ. *What Is Ignatian Spirituality?* (Loyola Press; Chicago), 2008.
- Ford, Michael. *Wounded Prophet: A Portrait of Henri J.M. Nouwen* (Doubleday),1999
- Foster, Richard J. *Sanctuary of the Soul: Journey into Meditative Prayer* (IVP: Downers Grove), 2011.
- Hafiz and Ladinsky, Daniel. *I Heard God Laughing: Poems of Hope and Joy* (Penguin), 2006.

- Ladinsky, Daniel, *Love Poems from God: Twelve Sacred Voices from the East and West* (Penguin), 2002.
- Keating, Thomas. *Open Mind, Open Heart.* (Warwick NY; Amity House), 1986.
- Meeter, Merle. *The Country of the Risen King: An Anthology of Christian Poetry* (baker Books; Ada), 1979.
- Merrill, Nan C. *Psalms for Praying: An Invitation to Wholeness* (Bloomsbury; London), 2006.
- Norris, Kathleen. *Acedia & me* (Riverhead Books; New York, 2008.
- Northumbria Community. *Celtic Daily Prayer* (HarperOne), 2002.
- Overton, Patrick. *The Leaning Tree,* (Bethany Press), 1975.
- Rilke, Rainer Maria. *Rilke's Book of Hours: Love Poems to God,* translated by Anita Barrows and Joanna Macy (Riverhead Books), 2005
- Roth, Geneen. *Women, Food and God* (Scribner; New York), 2011.
- Rumi. *Rumi: The Book of Love: Poems of Ecstasy and Longing* translated by Coleman Barks (HarperOne), 2005.
- Stewart, Mike. *No Crowds Present* (Fresh Wind Press; Abbotsford), 2007.
- Vanier, Jean and Hauerwas, Stanley. *Living Gently in a Violent World,* (InterVarsityPress; Downers Grove), 2008.
- Veltri, SJ, John Orientations. orientations.jesuits.ca

Music
- Geometric Shapes (Jeremy and Heidi Braacx). *View from My Hospital Bed,* (Bandcamp), 2011.
- Cockburn, Bruce. *The Charity of Night,* 1996.
- Mullins, Rich. *Songs,* 1996.

ACKNOWLEDGEMENTS

I'M THANKFUL THAT God set my heart on pilgrimage, and didn't send me off alone. Many have travelled with me, and they fill my heart with gratitude.

I will never forget the day I stumbled across Michael Cook's artwork while I was looking for an image to put on the spiritual direction page of my website. Asking Michael for permission to use *Burning Bush* led to more email conversations over the years. When I found *Night Prayer,* I knew I wanted it on the cover of my second book and *Seed Cracked Open* for the title. So I was thrilled when Daniel Ladinsky gave me permission to use the title and his translation of Hafiz's poems. I am thankful to Michael and Daniel for the love-mischief they and God do for the world.

I am also grateful for New Life Community Church, St. Stephen the Martyr Anglican Church, SoulStream, and Tri-Cities Imago Dei group, and my spiritual director, Karen Webber.

Thank you to Joy Richardson who put together two of the prayer retreat outlines, Eileen Kernaghan and the Kyle Writers' Group who gave me feedback on many of these stories before they were published, and Farida Somjee and Ceri Polderman for proofreading.

I would have given up long ago if I hadn't been so blessed with such encouraging words from my readers who told me how they have been impacted by what I write. Thank you, dear reader!

I am especially grateful for my husband, Fred. Before each post is published he reads it over and gives me feedback. I love it when he smiles and says, "It's great. I wouldn't change a thing." But it's even better when he can bravely point out a missing word or a sentence that just doesn't make sense. Fred, you're the best.

ABOUT THE AUTHOR

ESTHER HIZSA LIVES in Burnaby, B.C., with her husband, Fred. She has a Master of Divinity degree from Regent College, Vancouver, B.C. and worked for over twenty years as an associate pastor—first in the United Church of Canada and then in the Canadian Reformed Church in America. She offers spiritual direction (trained through SoulStream) and co-facilitates SoulStream's spiritual formation course, Living from the Heart. Her writing has been published in *Journey toward Home: Soul Travel from Advent to Lent* (edited by Kristin Carroccino and Christine Sine); *Pacific Yachting* and *Mennonite Herald* magazines; Au coeur du monde: Des Chemins de Dialogue, *Journal of Ignatian Spirituality 2018/19* and various blogs, including her own, *An Everyday Pilgrim.* Her first book, *Stories of an Everyday Pilgrim,* was published in 2015. This is her second.

Esther loves camping and bike riding with Fred, her monthly Scrabble night with friends (especially when she wins), and playing Sardines in the Dark with Fred and their grandchildren, Hadrian and Hannah.

Visit *An Everyday Pilgrim* at www.estherhizsa.com

READERS' COMMENTS ABOUT
SEED CRACKED OPEN

"It always seems I can take away something from your writing and apply it to my life."—Melanie

"Thanks for being honest in what you're going through. The perspective you give helps a lot."—Donna

"Oh Esther, what you wrote is beautiful. A big part of your gift is your vulnerability."—Karen

"Esther, love it, love it, love it! Thanks for your timely insights into my own little messes!"—Liane

"Love your God—so accessible and personal. I wish I had known your God when I was young."—Valerie

"Thank you for your amplification of the Bible and for your insights about how to shift our hurts. I find your writing down to earth, well-grounded in reality and helpful. I also appreciate your willingness to write in the first person and let me know you better."—Jan

"I've been very restless and excited this past month preparing to move into a new home. Your writing was a reminder that I am in the Lord's hand."—Cheryl

"Esther, this caught my breath—oh my! My eyes fill with tears, such tenderness, such love! Thank you for sharing."—Gail

"Thank you for adding a little more fuel to that Holy Lamp within my heart."—Jim